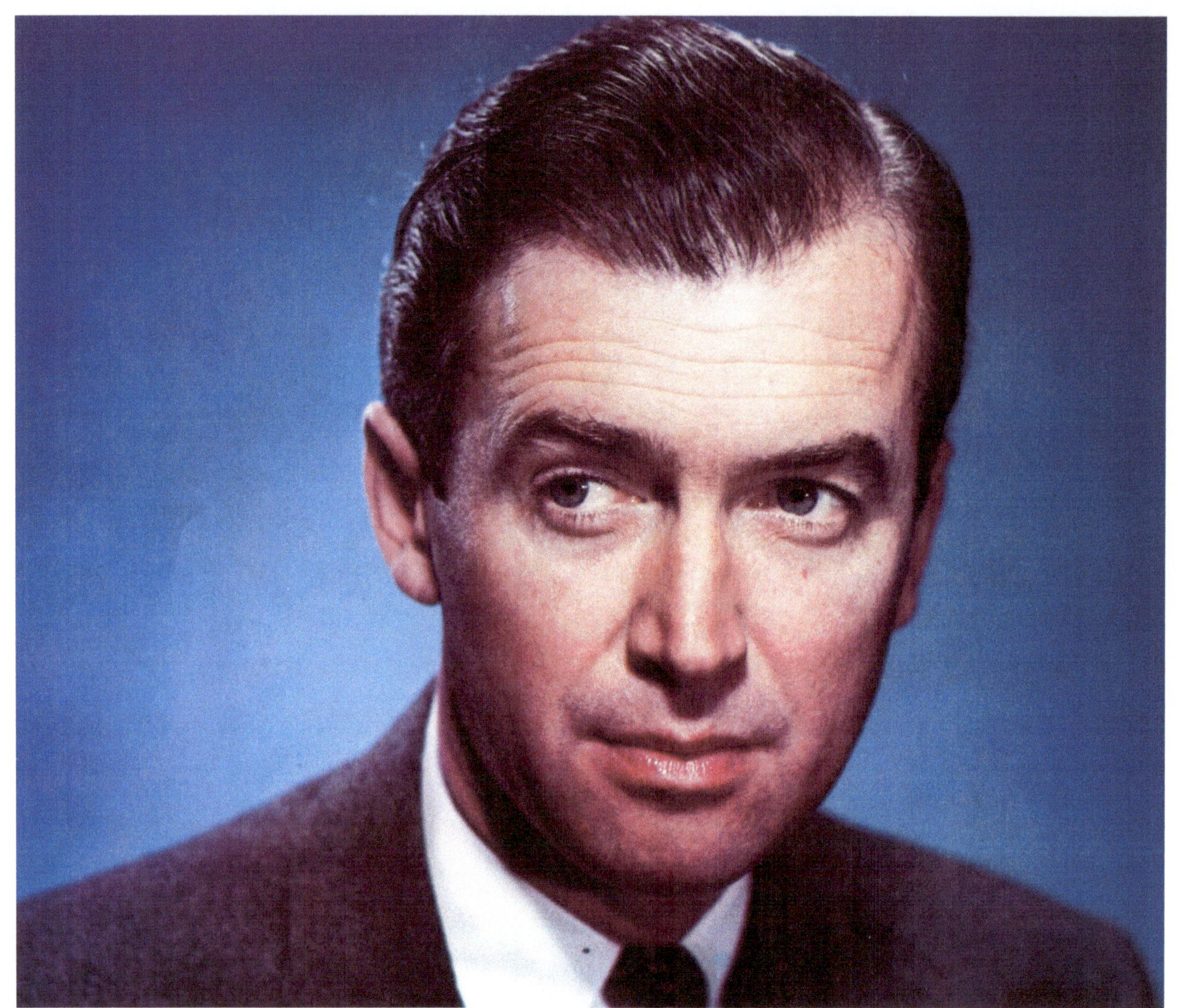

James Stewart

Movies:

- It's A Wonderful Life
- Vertigo
- The Philadelphia Story
- Rear Window

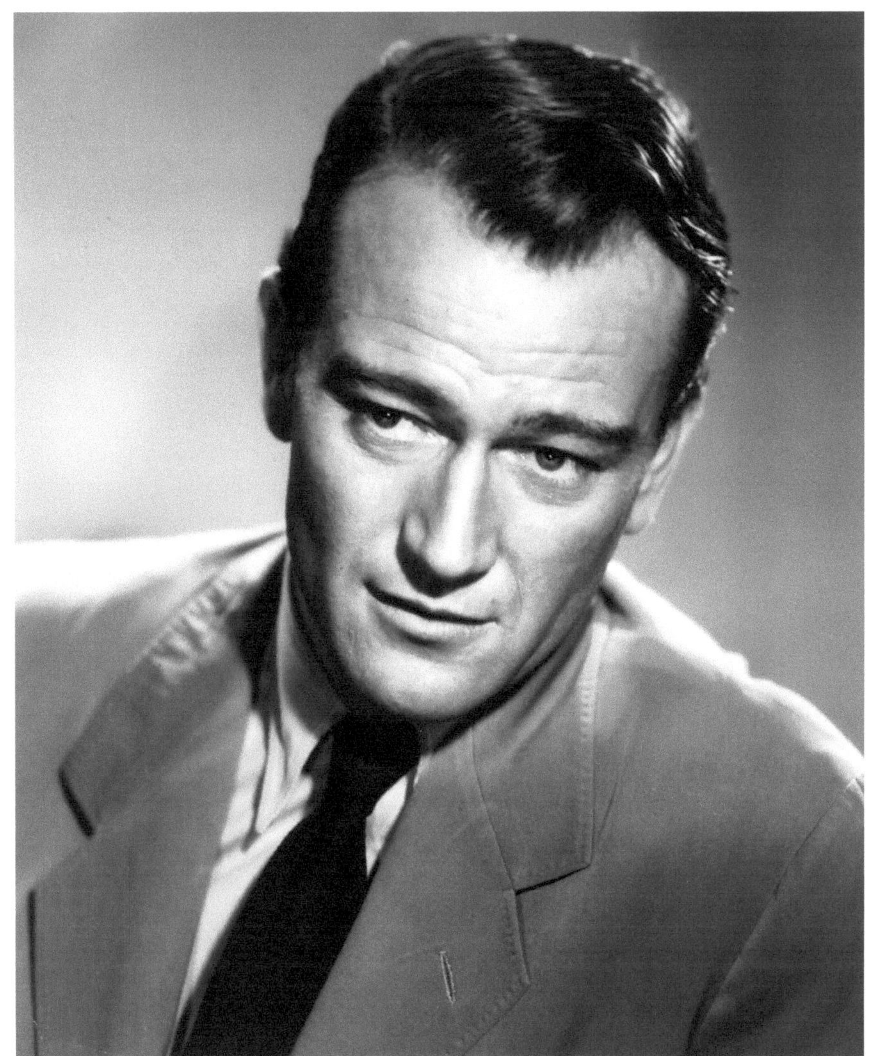

John Wayne

Movies:

- The Searchers
- Stage Coach
- Rio Bravo
- Red River

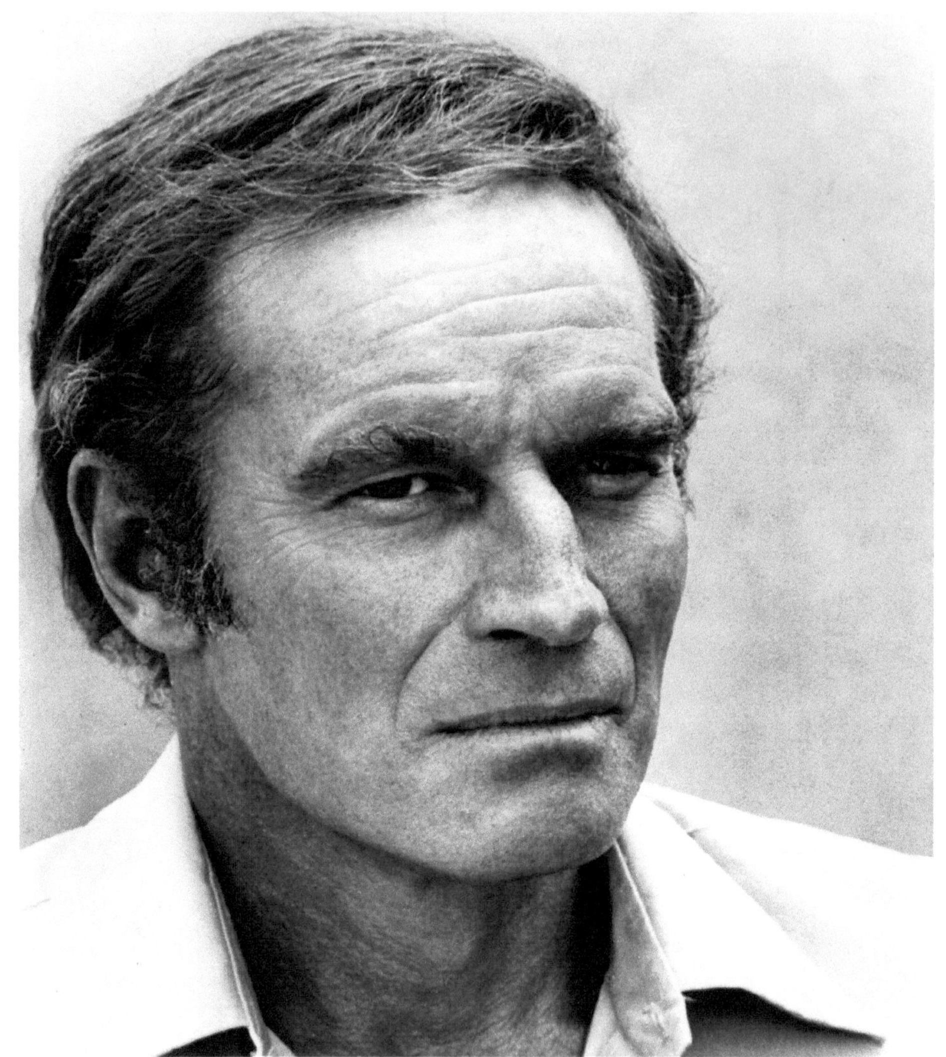

Charlton Heston

Movies:

- Ben-Hur
- The Ten Commandments
- Planet of Apes
- Soylent Green

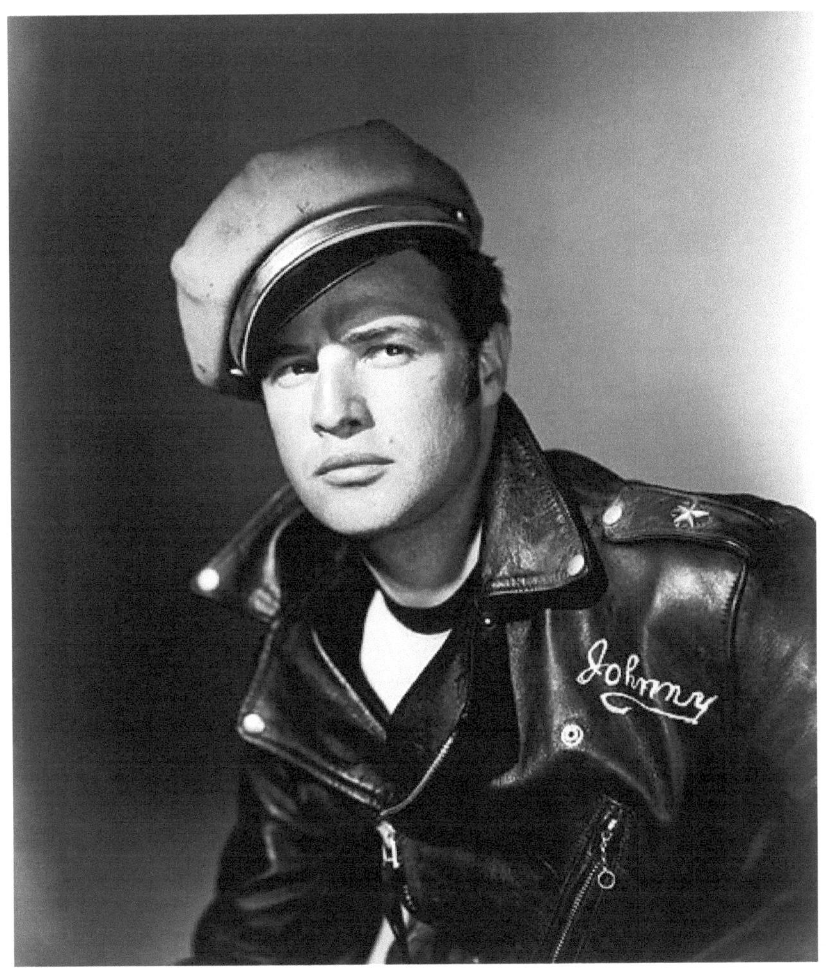

Marlon Brando

Movies:

- The Godfather
- Superman
- Apocalypse Now
- On The Waterfront

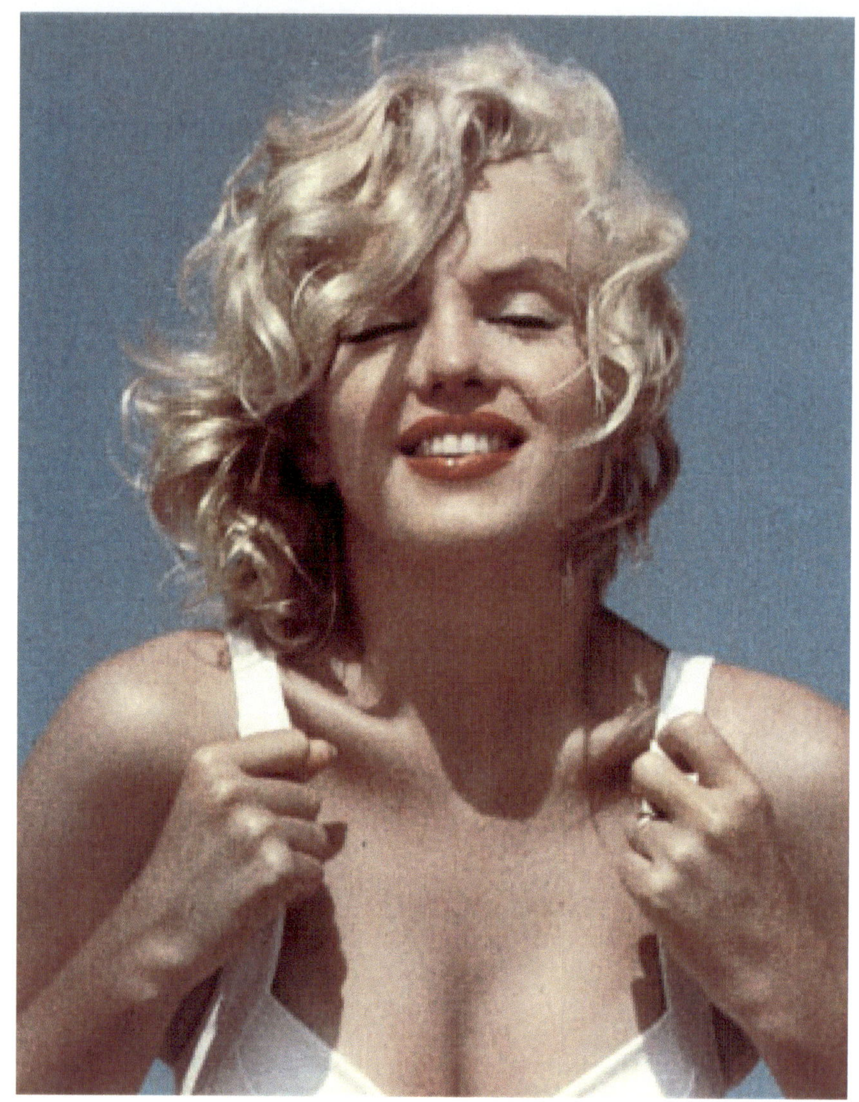

Marilyn Monroe

Movies:

- Some Like It Hot
- All About Eve
- The Misfits
- The Seven Year Itch

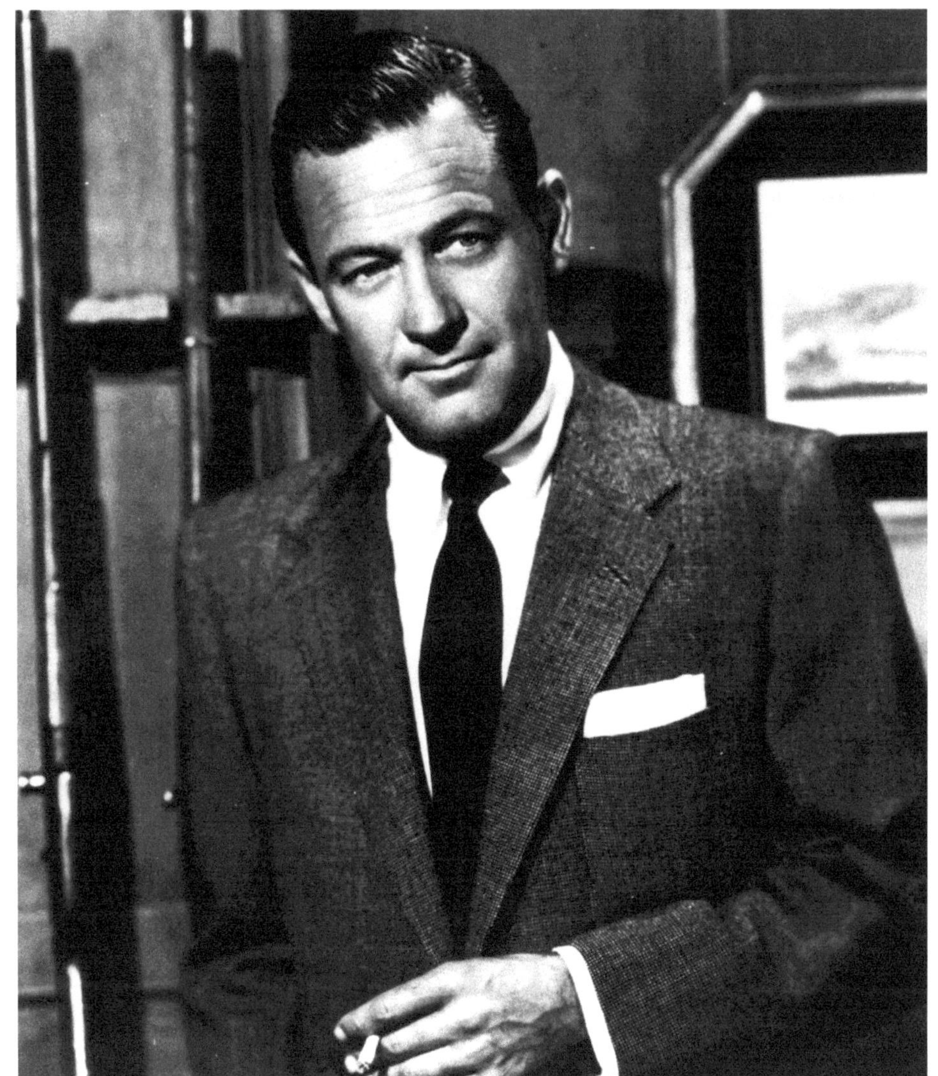

William Holden

Movies:

- Sunset Blvd.
- Sabrina
- Breezy
- Stalag 17

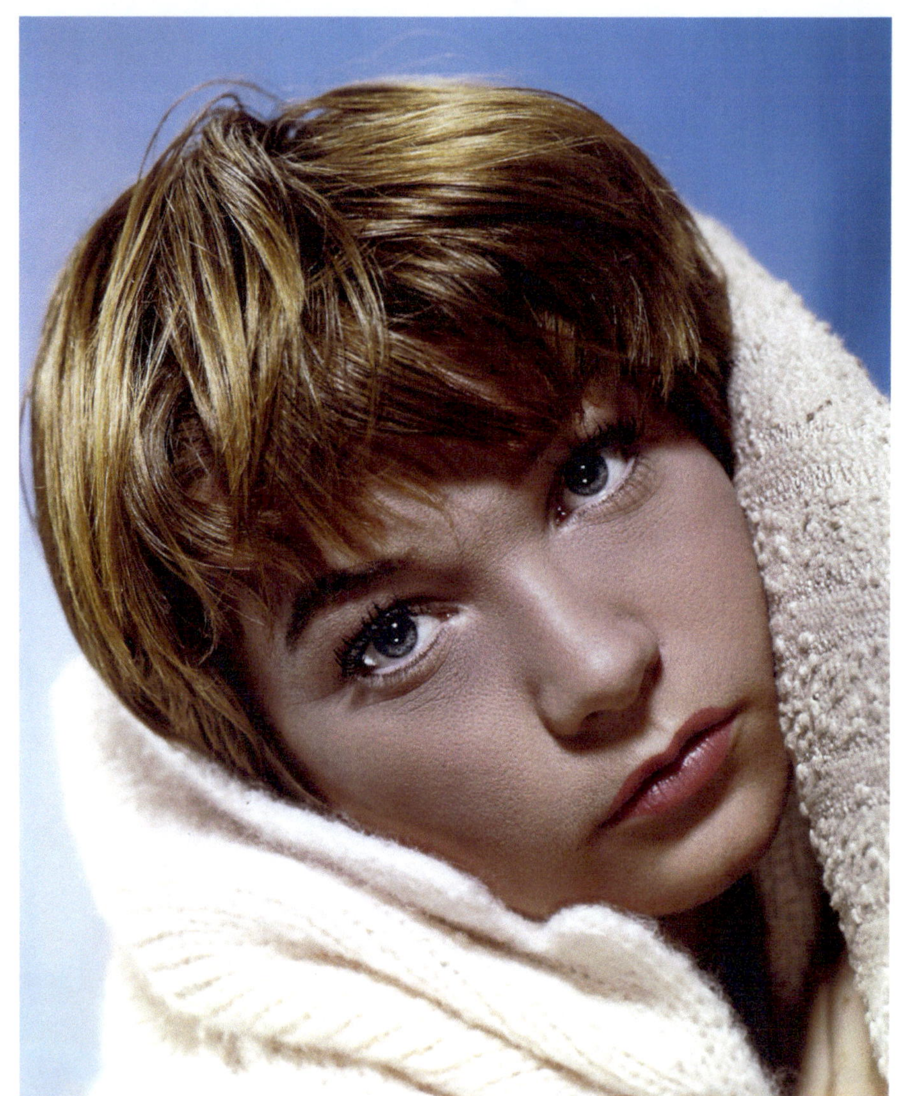

Shirley MacLaine

Movies:

- The Apartment
- Being There
- Steel Magnolias
- Valentine's Day

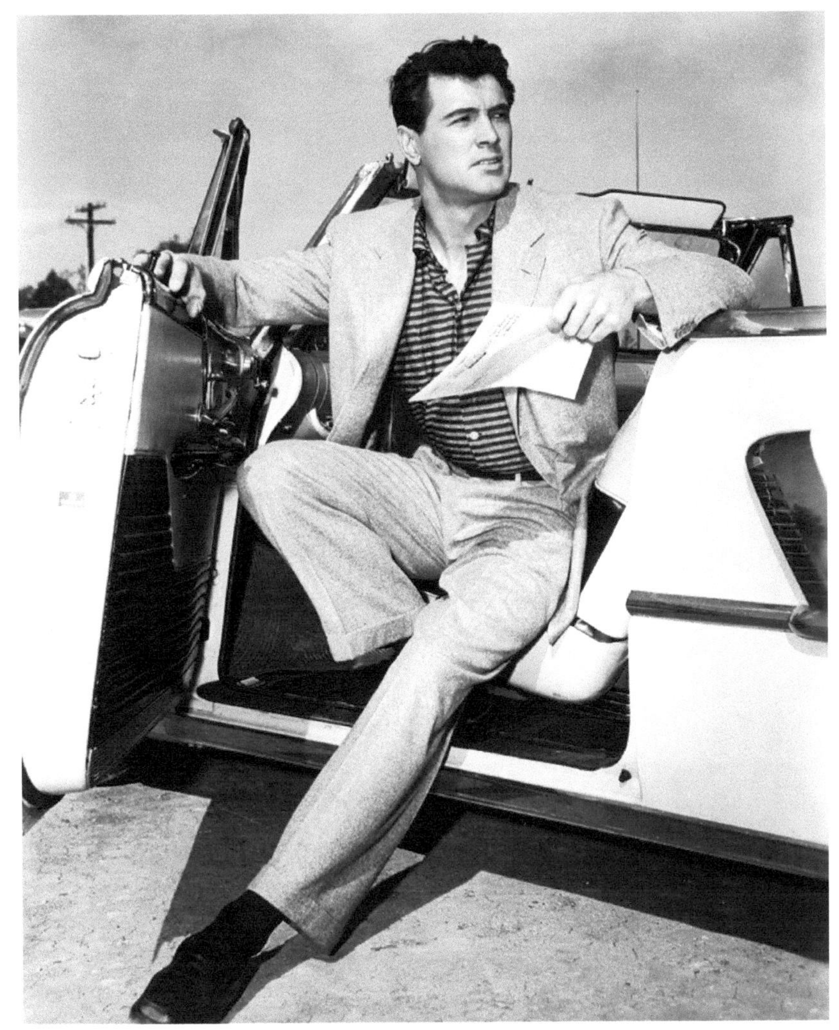

Rock Hudson

Movies:

- Giant
- All That Heaven Allows
- Pillow Talk
- Lover Come Back

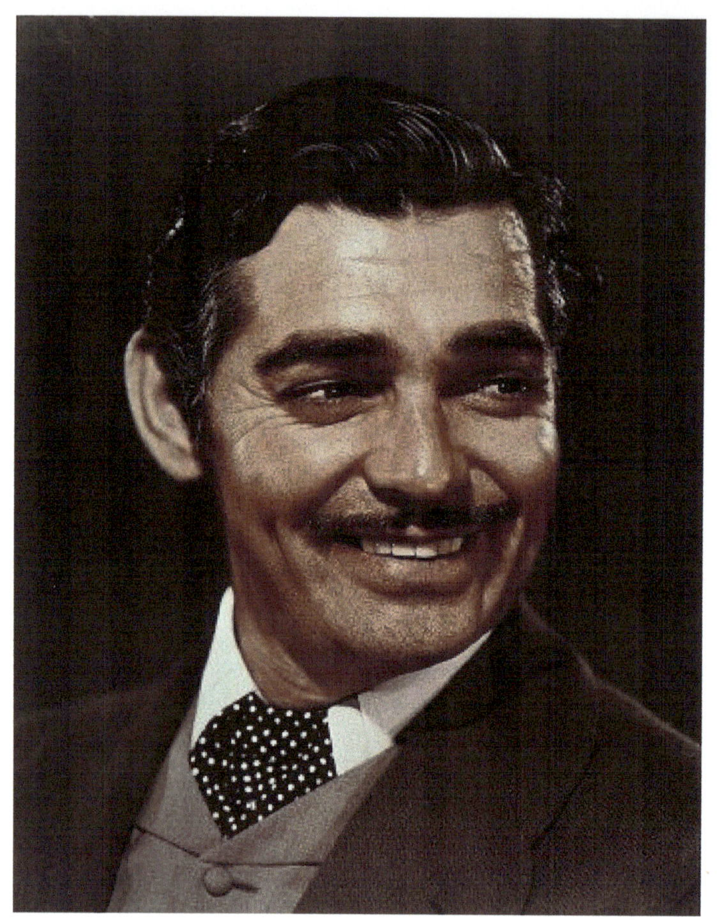

Clark Gable

Movies:

- Gone With The Wind
- It Happened One Night
- The Misfits
- Cinema Paradiso

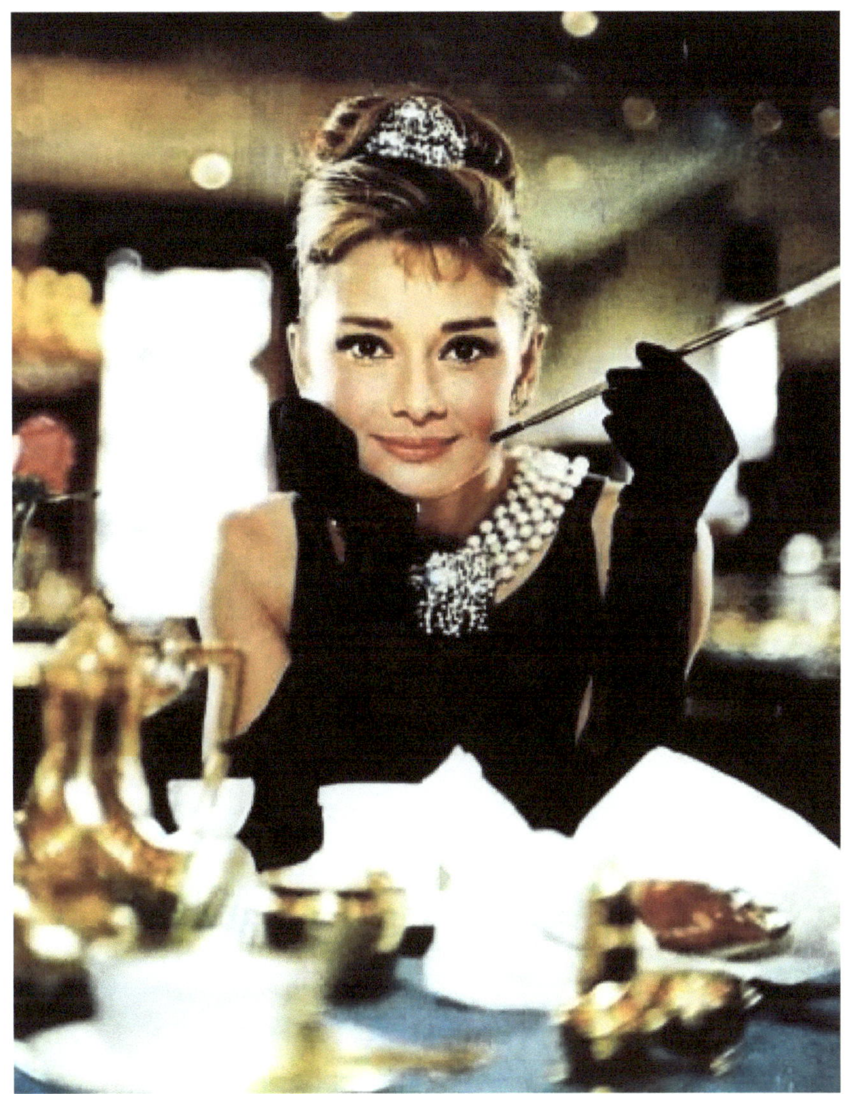

Audrey Hepburn

Movies:

- Breakfast At Tiffany's
- Roman Holiday
- My Fair Lady
- Charade

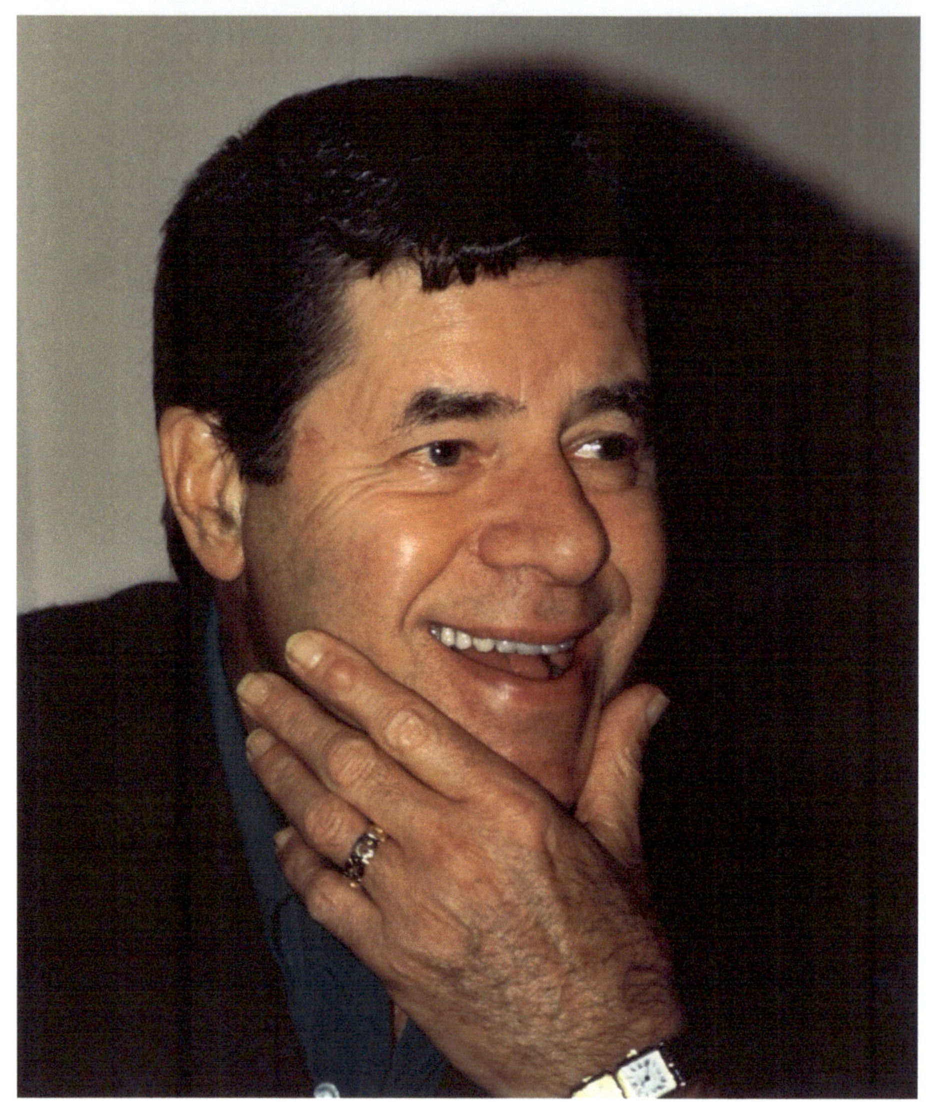

Jerry Lewis

Movies:

- The Nutty Professor
- The King of Comedy
- The Ladies Man
- The Family Jewels

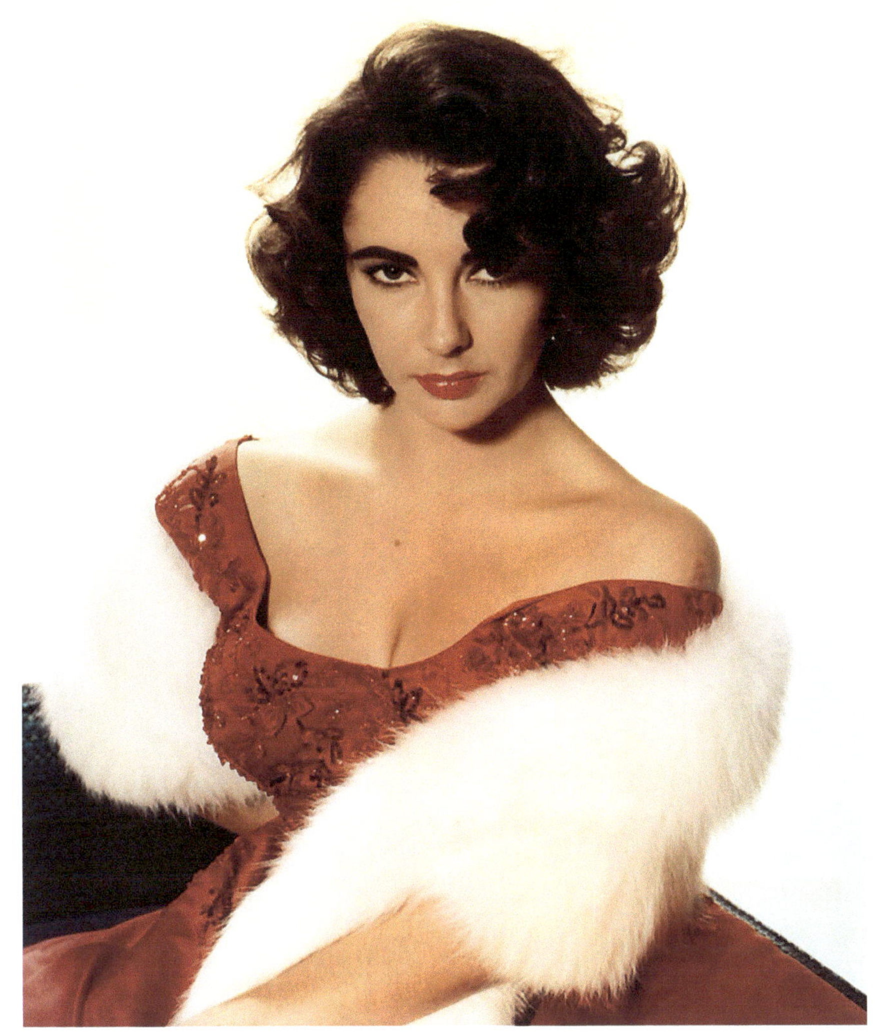

Elizabeth Taylor

Movies:

- Cleopatra
- National Velvet
- The Flintstones
- Giant

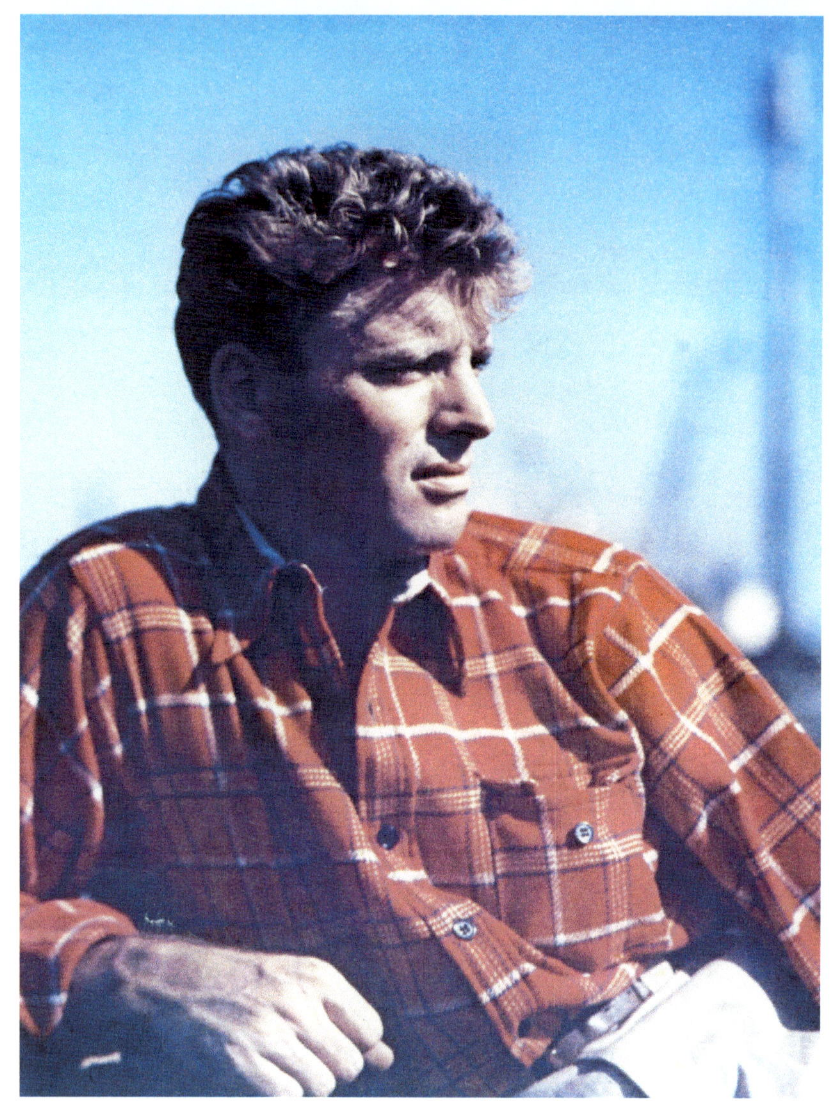

Burt Lancaster

Movies:

- Elmer Gantry
- Sweet Smell of Success
- From Here to Eternity
- The Killers

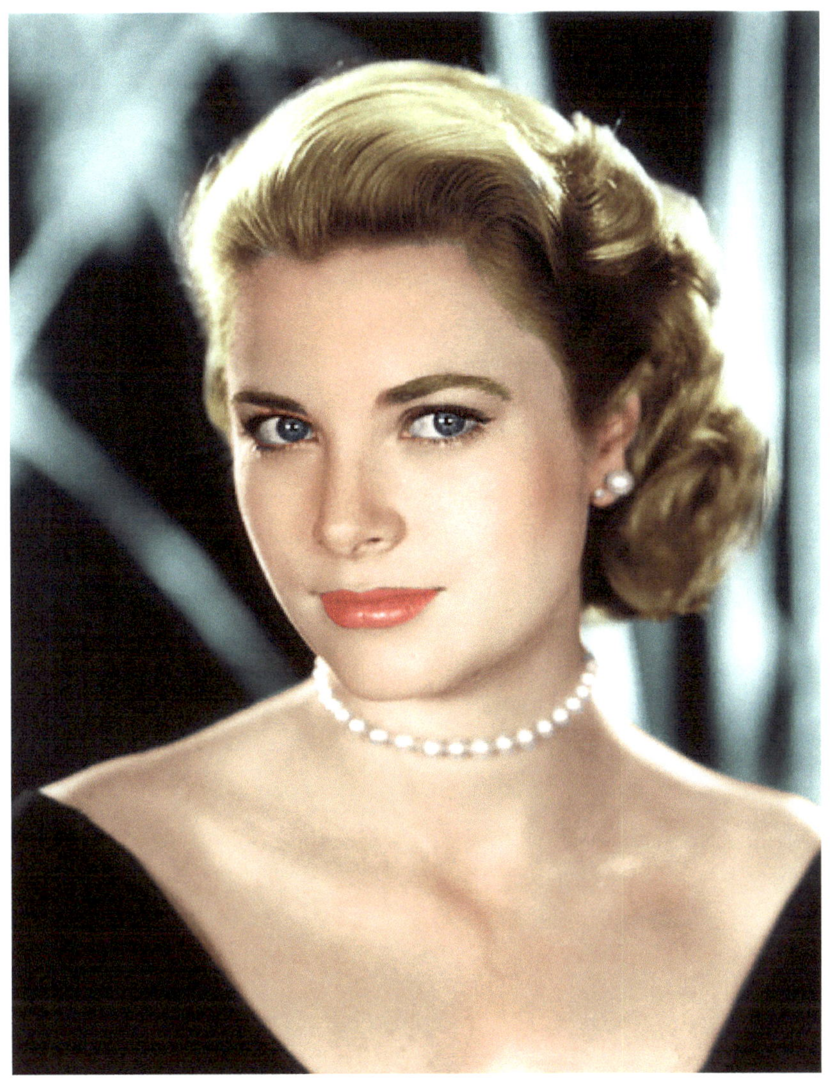

Grace Kelly

Movies:

- Rear Window
- To Catch a Thief
- High Noon
- Dial M for Murder

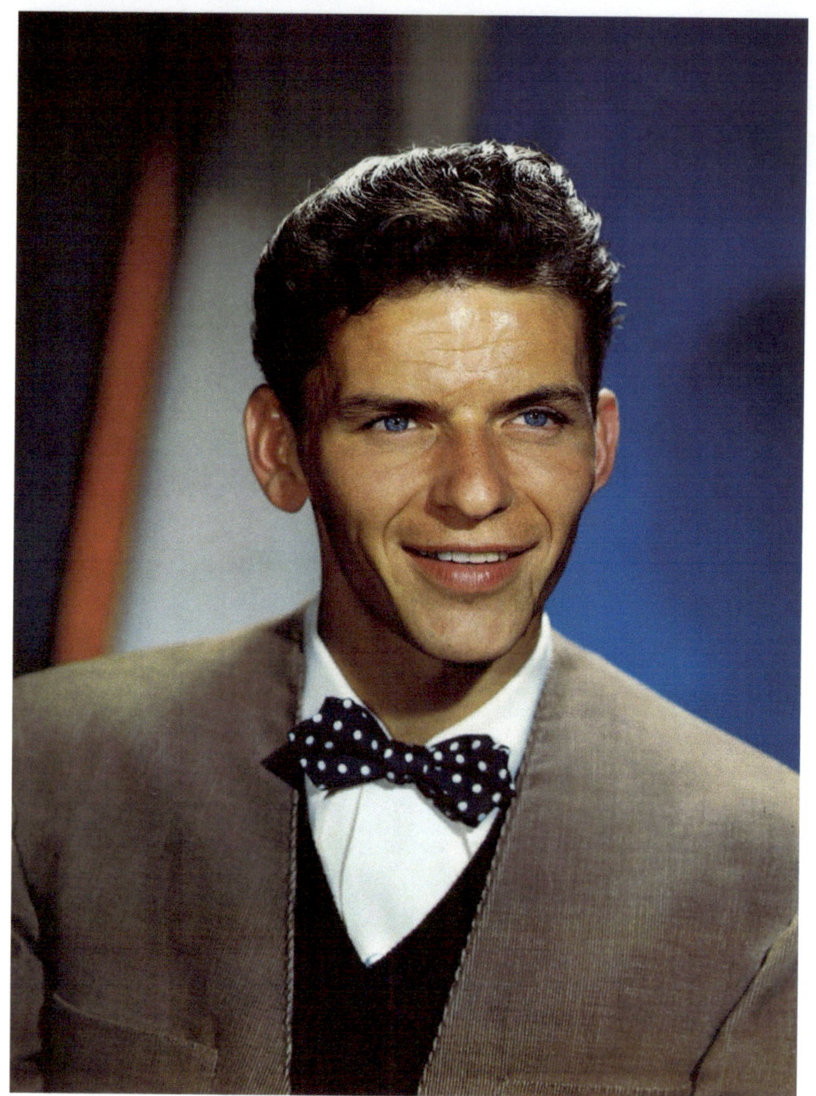

Frank Sinatra

Movies:

- From Here To Eternity
- Anchors Aweigh
- Ocean's Eleven
- On The Town

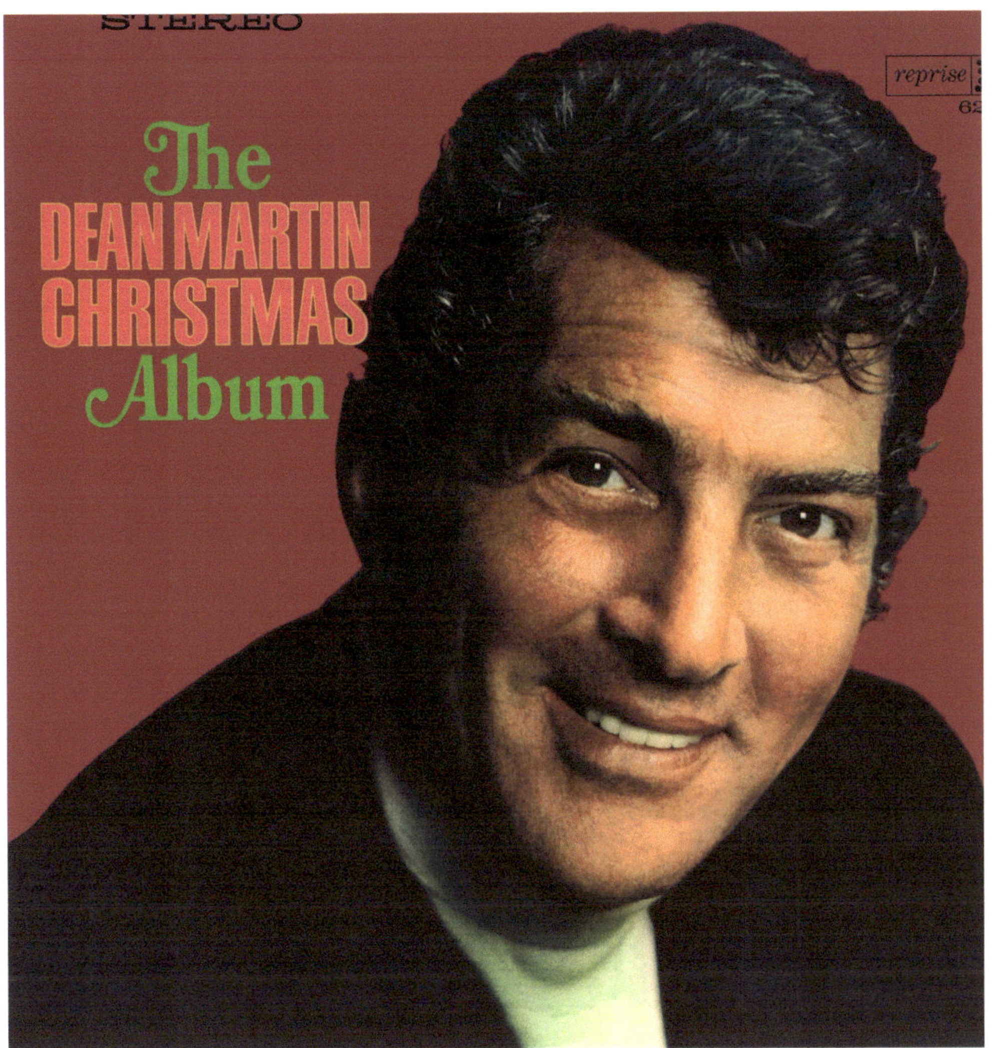

Dean Martin

Movies:

- Rio Bravo
- Some Came Running
- The Young Lions
- Sailor Beware

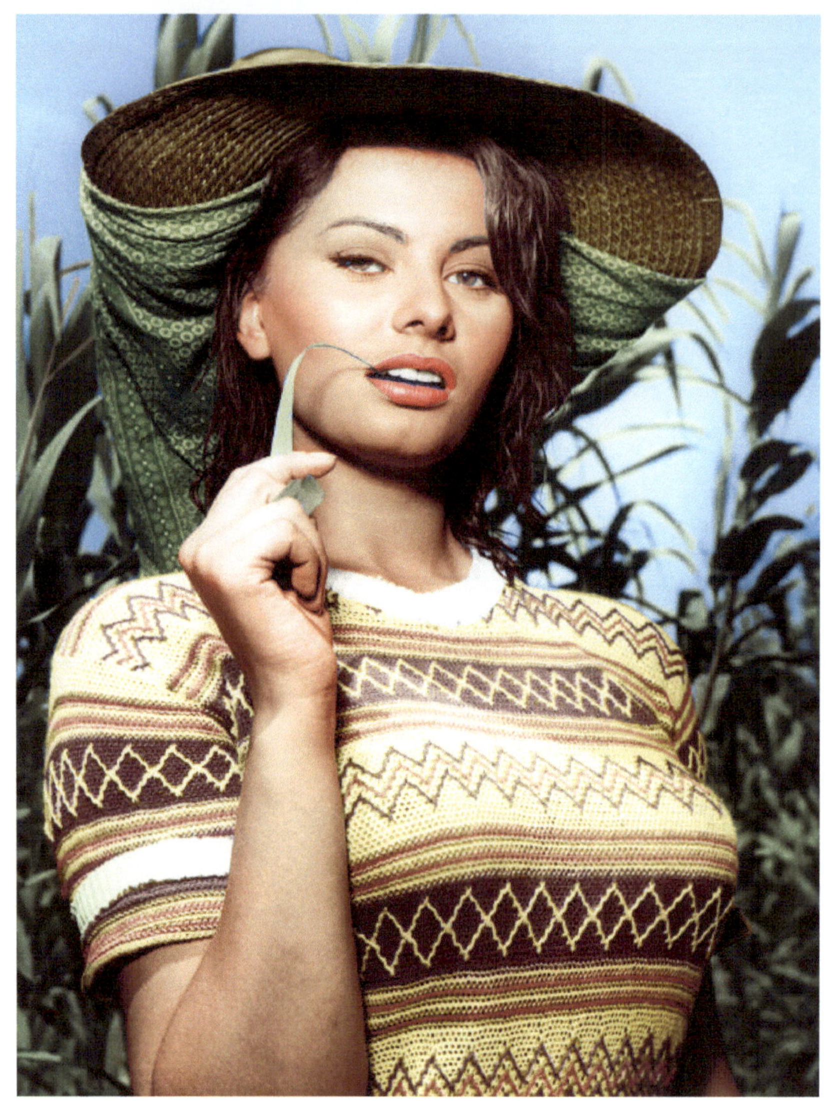

Sophia Loren

Movies:

- El Cid
- Nine
- The Cassandra Crossing
- A Special Day

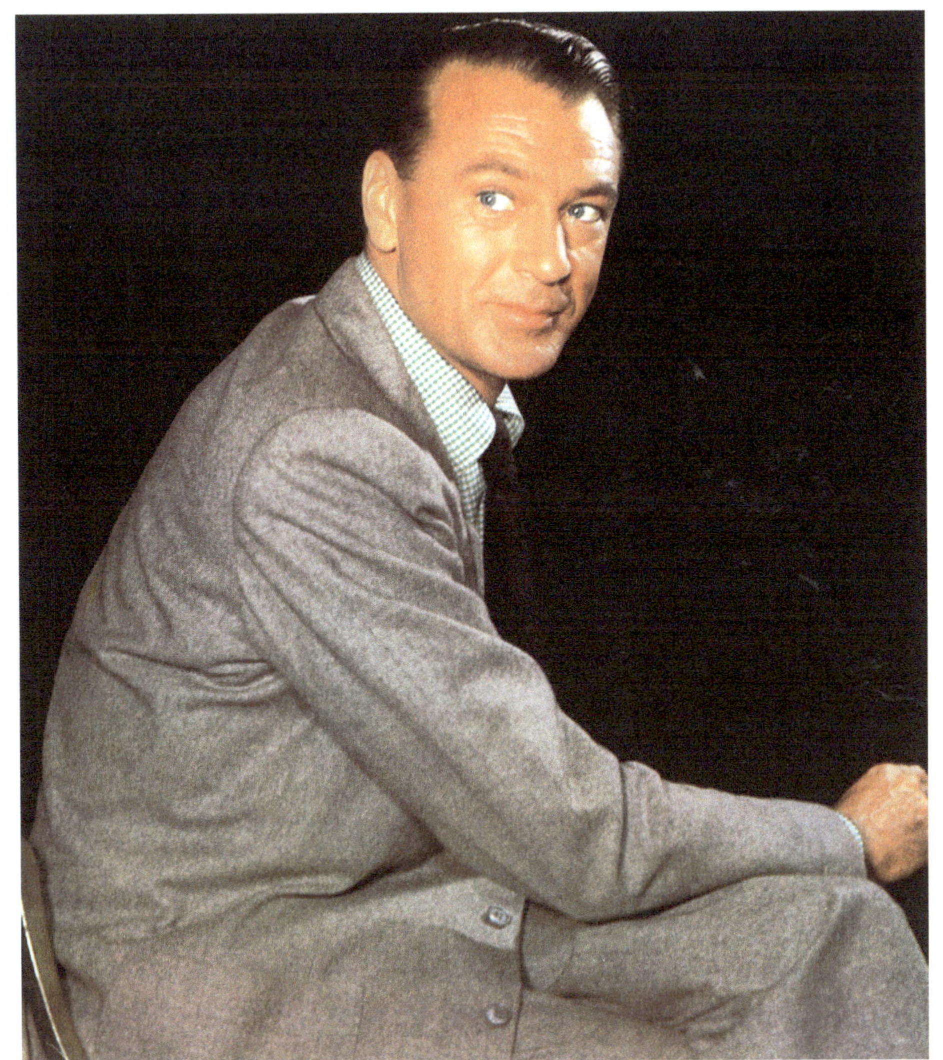

Gary Cooper

Movies:

- High Noon
- Cinema Paradiso
- Mr. Deeds Goes to Town
- Wings

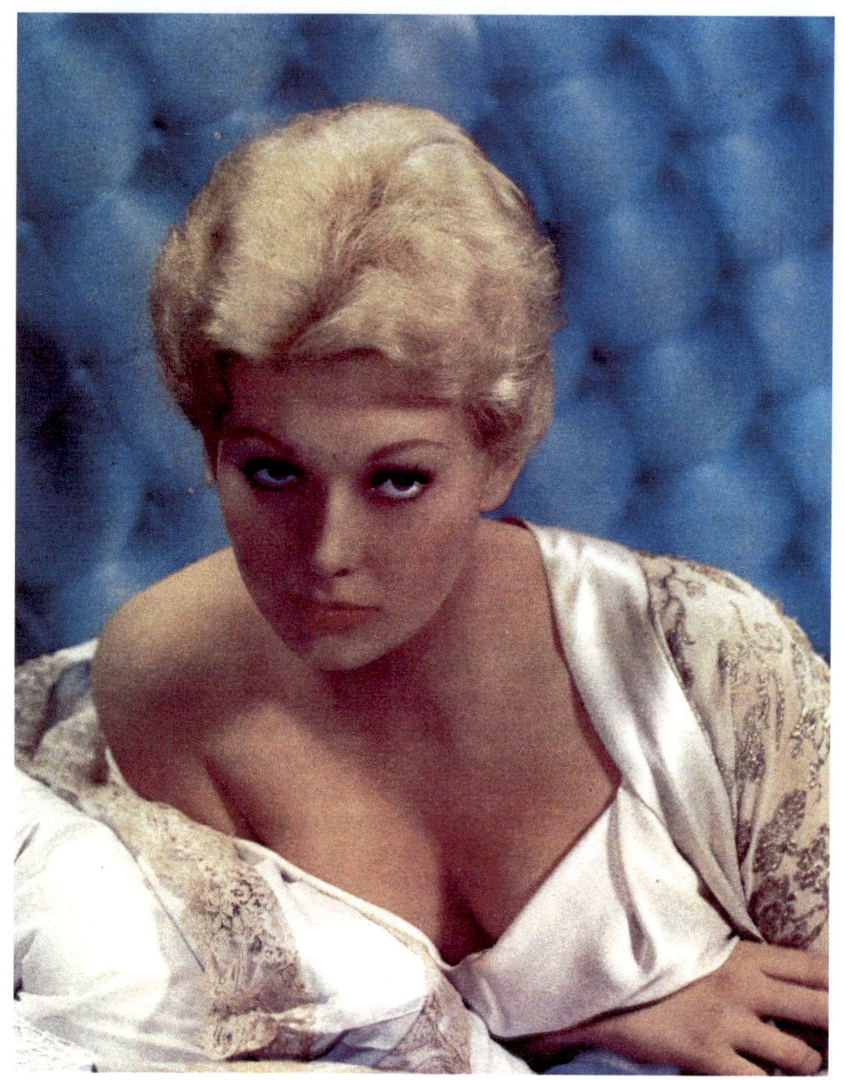

Kim Novak

Movies:

- Vertigo
- Book and Candle
- Bell
- Picnic

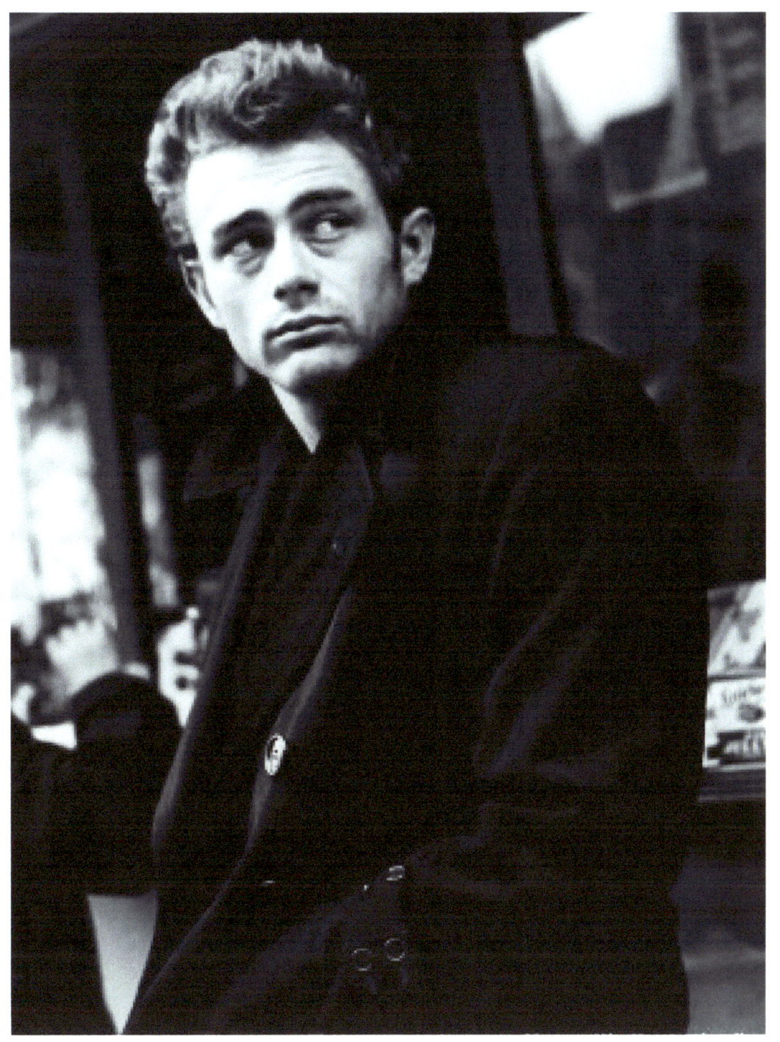

James Dean

Movies:

- Rebel Without a Cause
- Giant
- East of Eden
- Sailor Beware

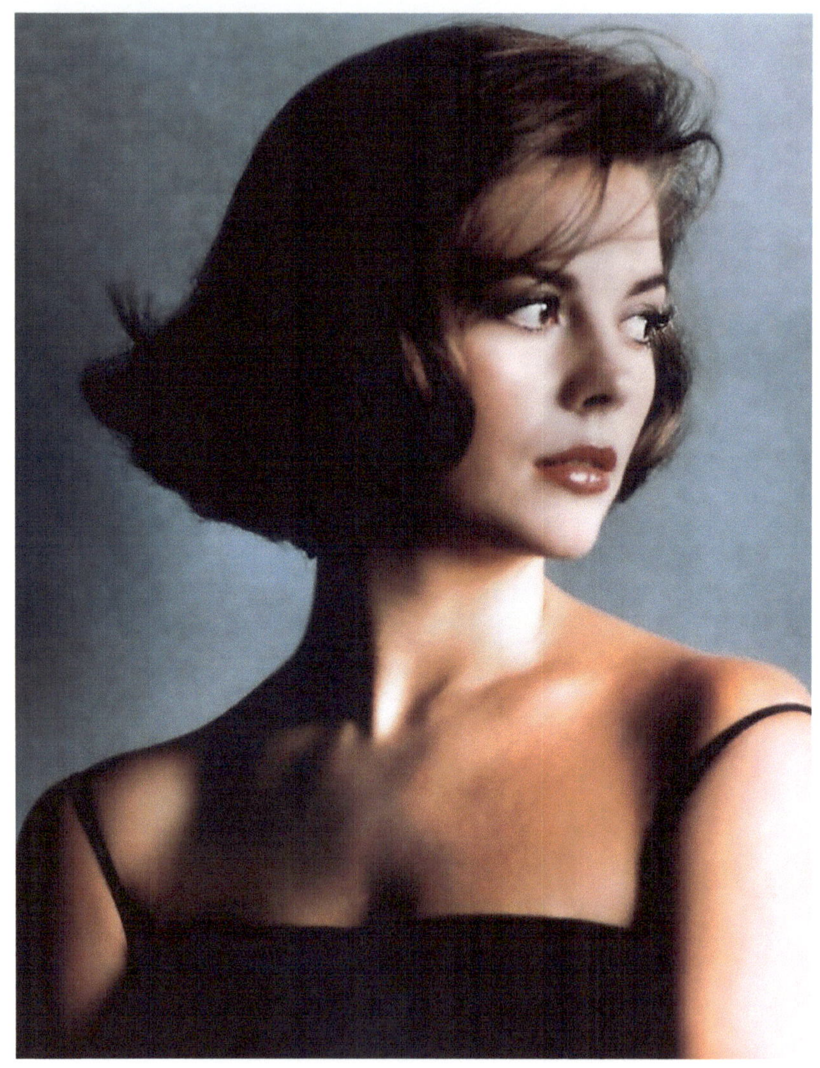

Natalie Wood

Movies:

- West Side Story
- Miracle on 34th Street
- Rebel Without a Cause
- The Searchers

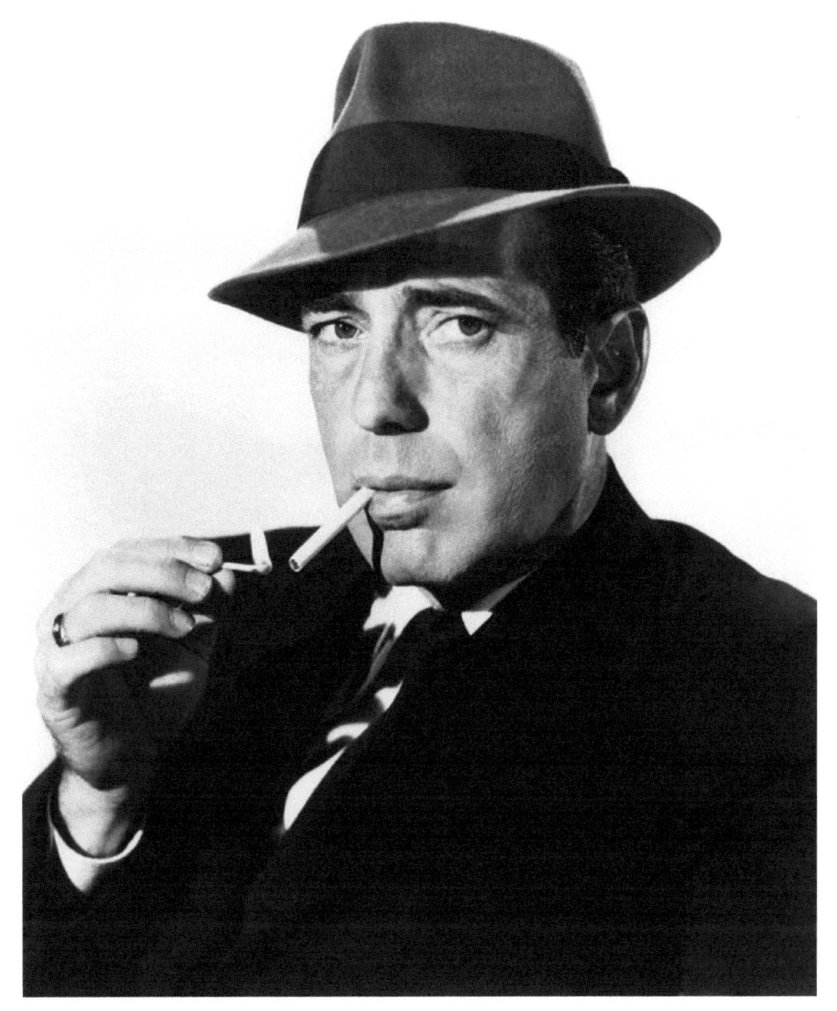

Humphrey Bogart

Movies:

- Casablanca
- The Maltese Falcon
- The African Queen
- The Big Sleep

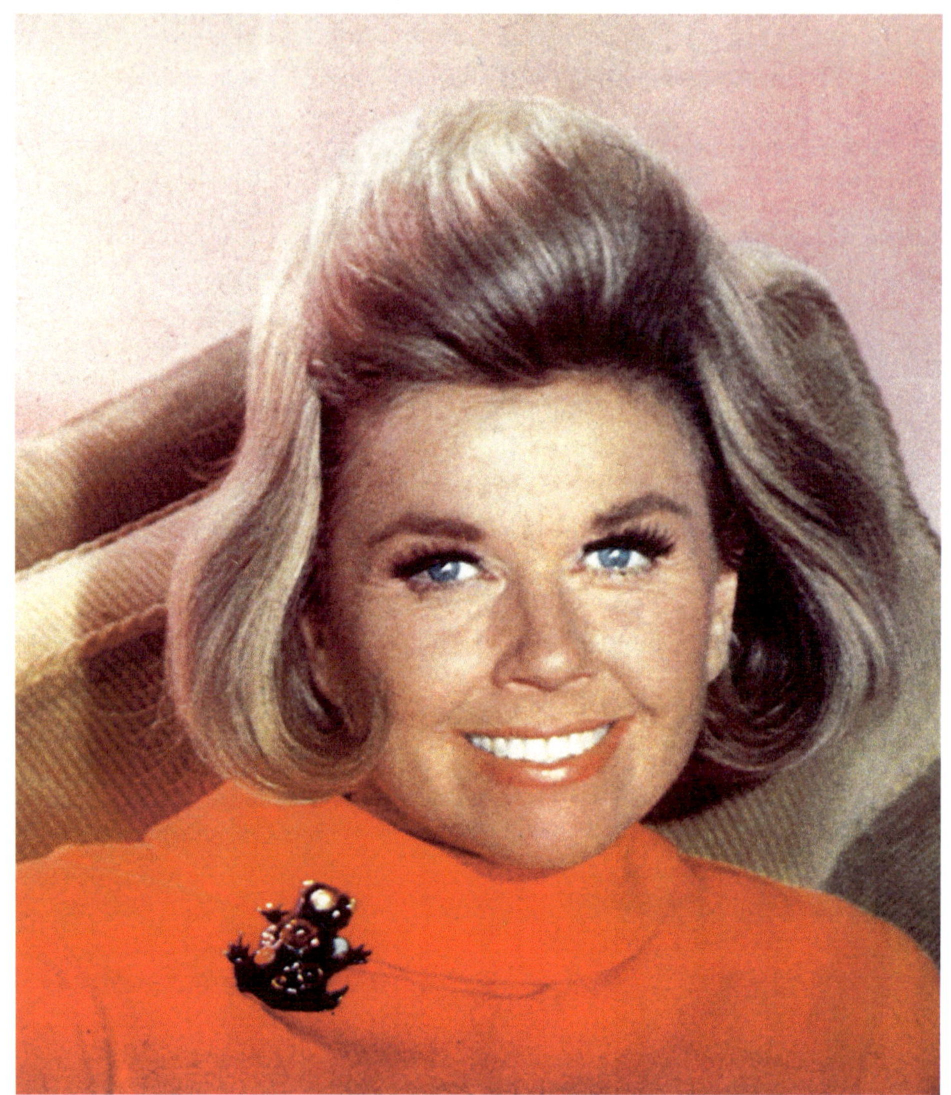

Doris Day

Movies:

- Pillow Talk
- Calamity Jane
- Lover Come Back
- Move Over

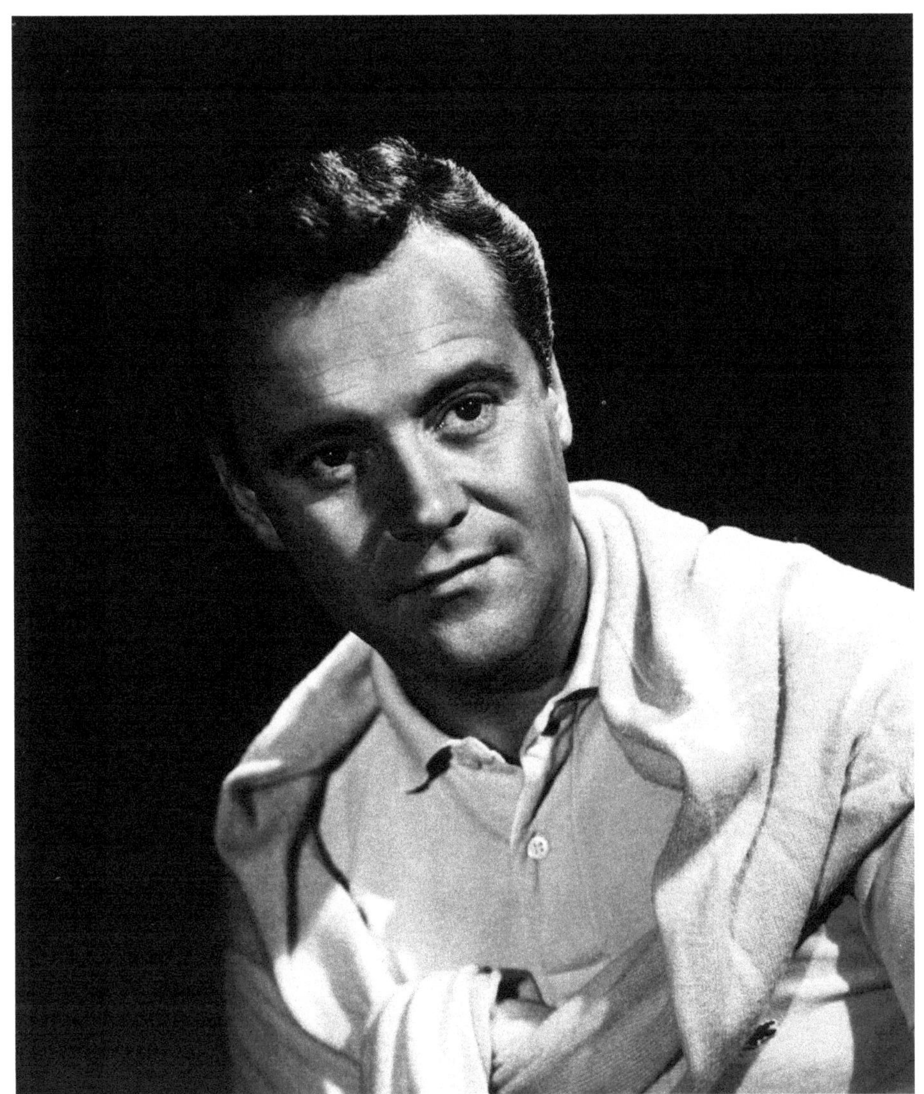

Jack Lemmon

Movies:

- Some Like It Hot
- The Apartment
- JFK
- Grumpy Old Men

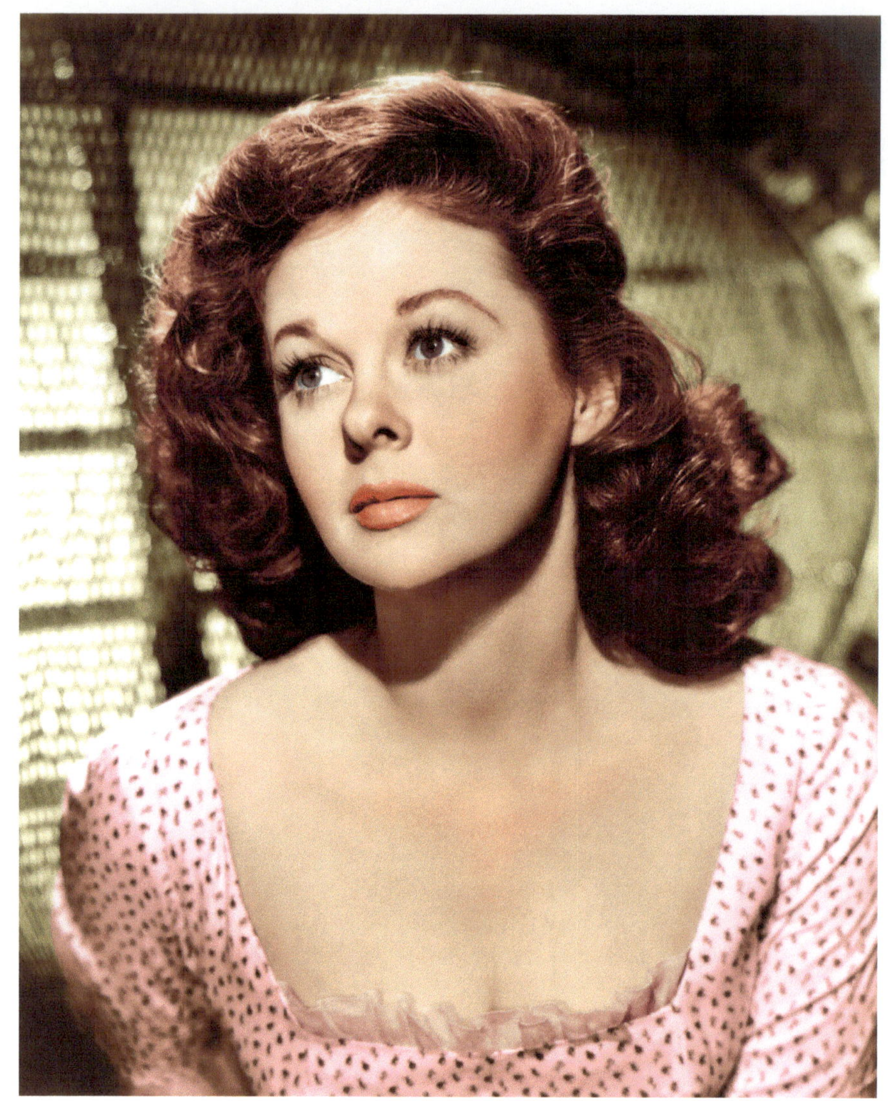

Susan Hayward

Movies:

- I Want to Live!
- Valley of the Dolls
- Garden of Evil
- The Lusty Men

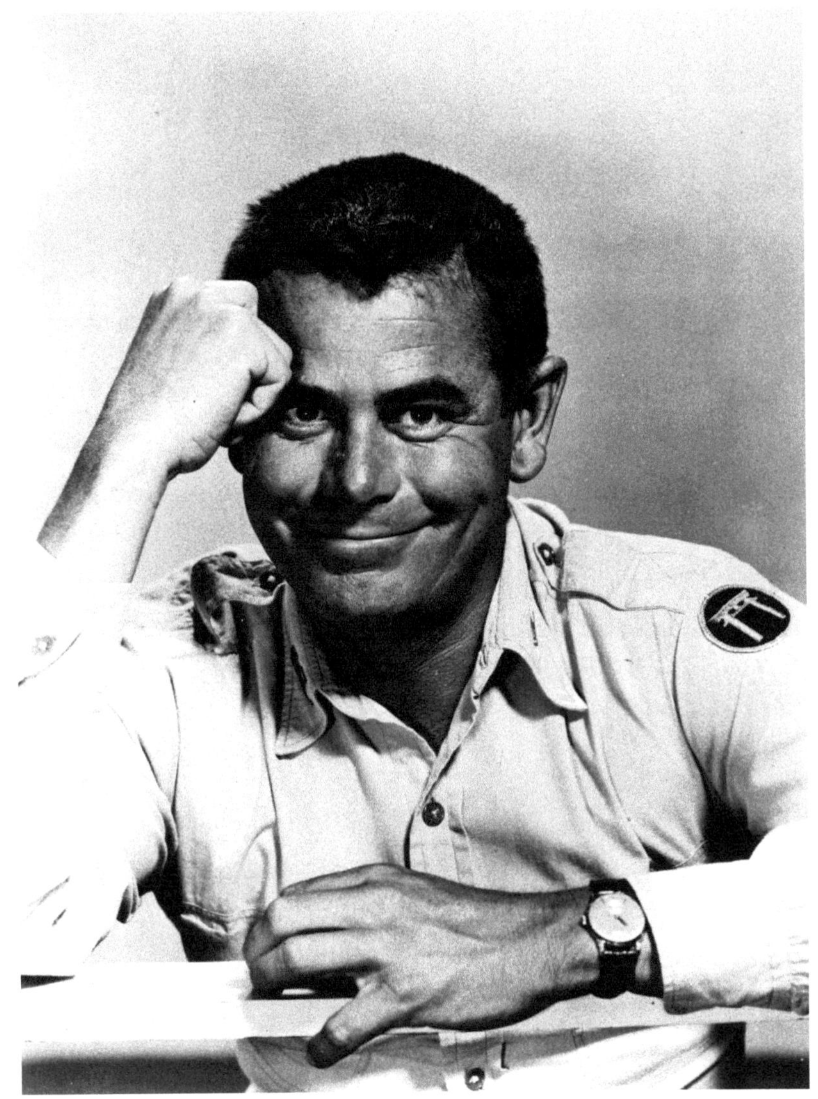

Glenn Ford

Movies:

- Gilda
- Blackboard Jungle
- A Stolen Life
- Superman II

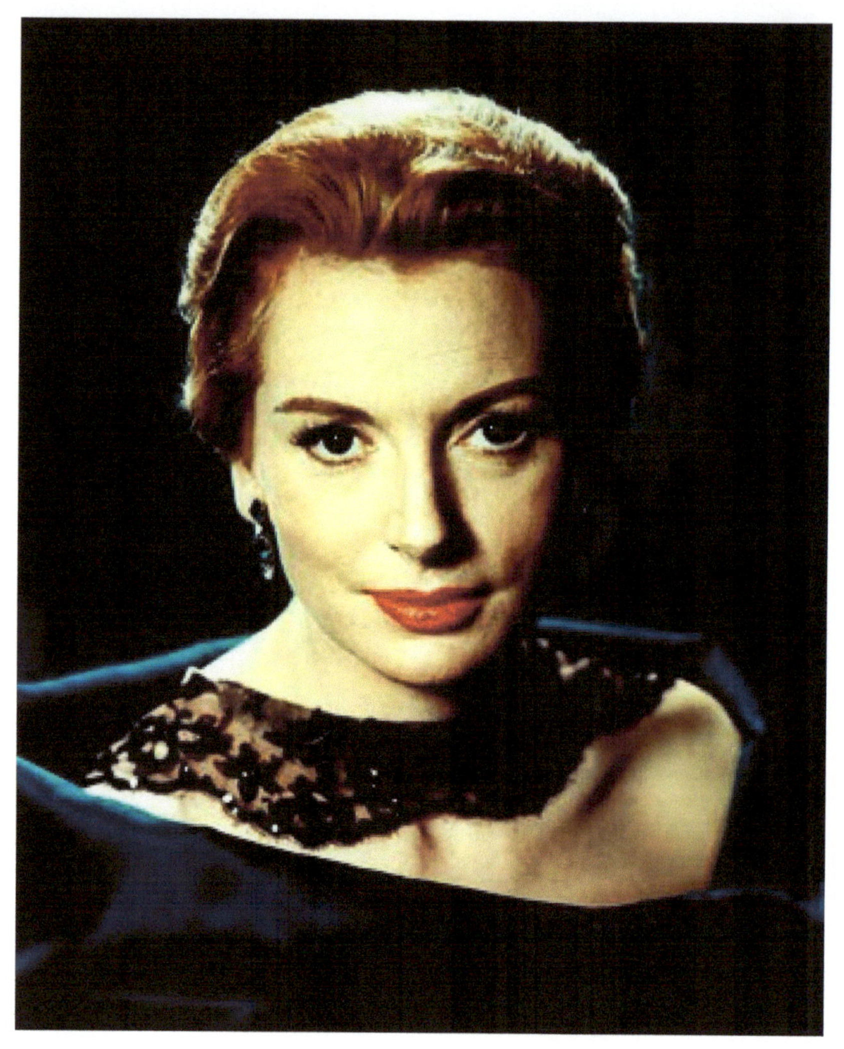

Deborah Kerr

Movies:

- An Affair To Remember
- The King and I
- Quo Vadis
- Separate Tables

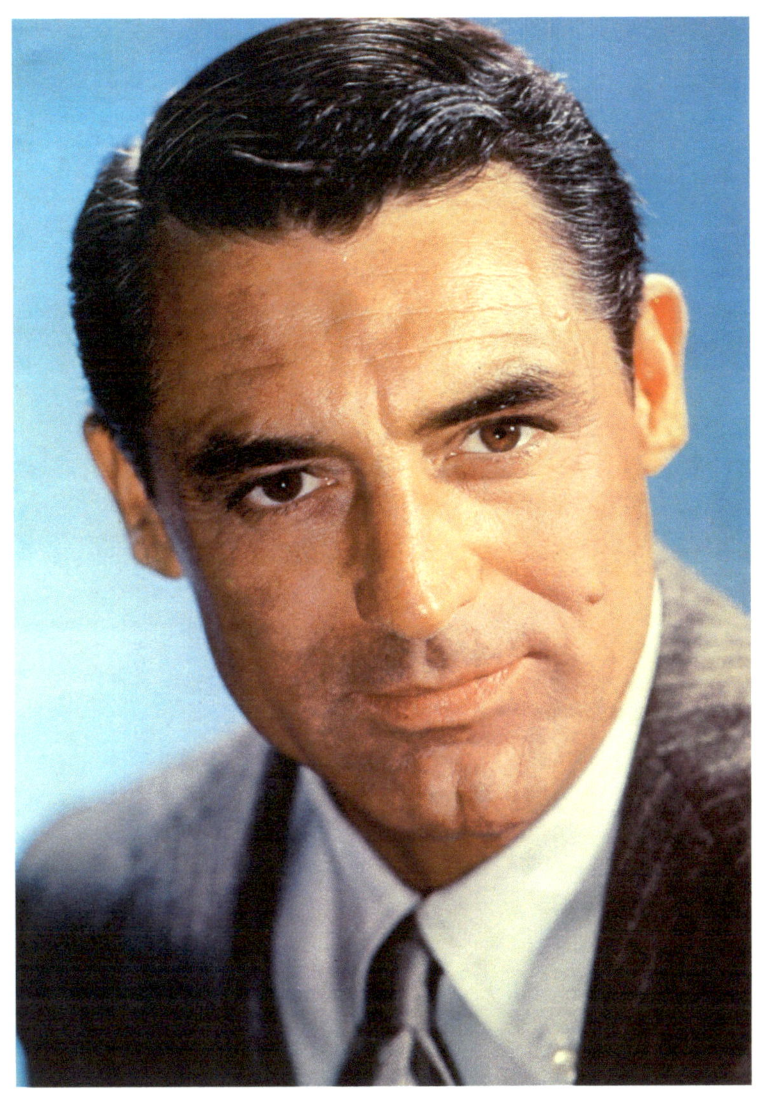

Cary Grant

Movies:

- North by Northwest
- Suzy
- She done Him Wrong
- I'm No Angel

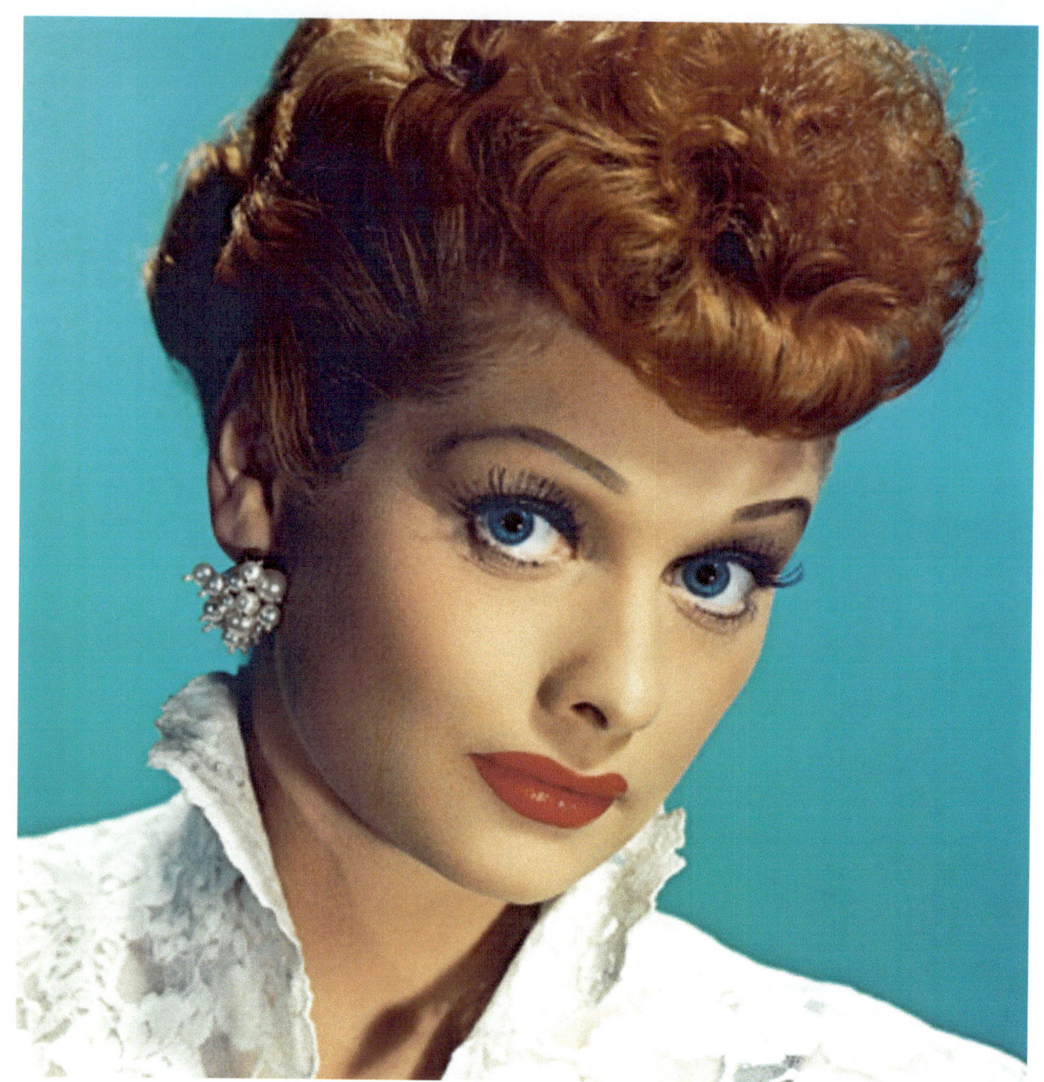

Lucille Ball

Movies:

- All the Right Moves
- Stage Door
- Top Hat
- Room Service

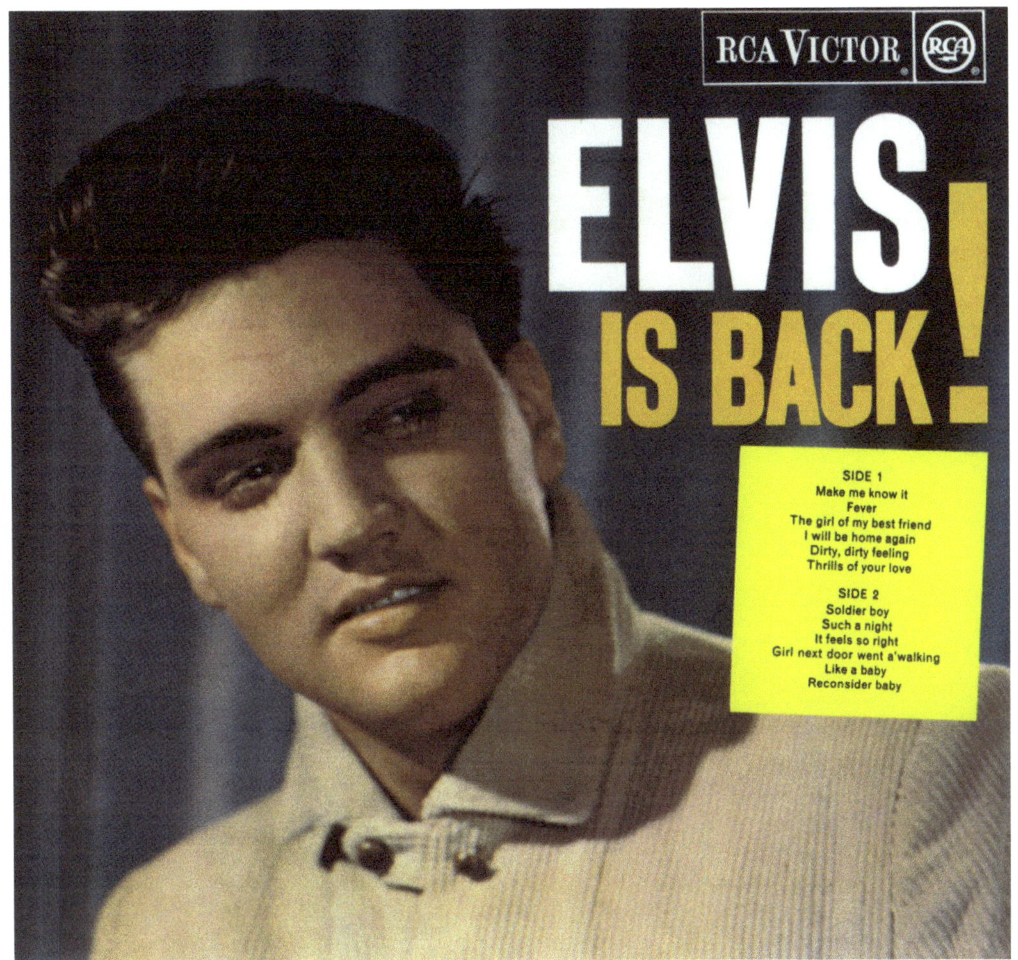

Elvis Presley

Movies:

- Love Me Tender
- Loving You
- Jailhouse Rock
- G.I. Blues

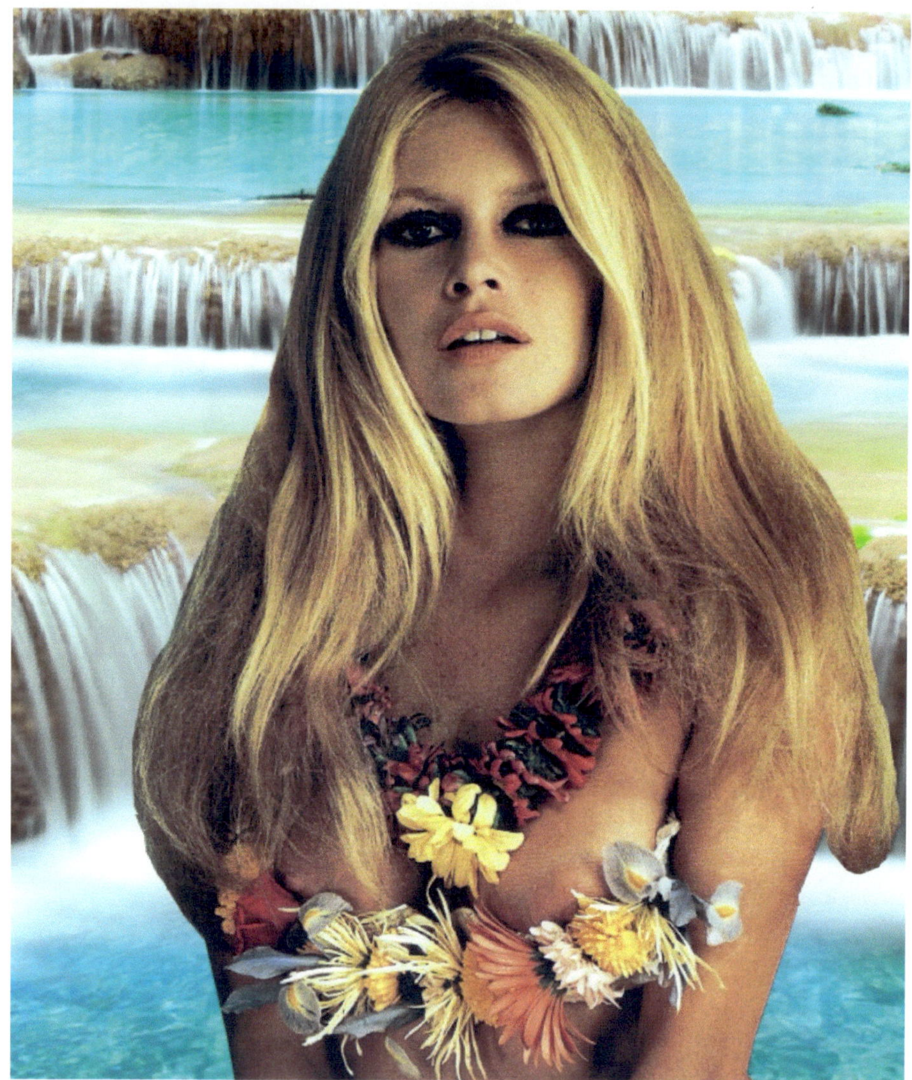

Brigitte Bardot

Movies:

- Cinema Paradiso
- Contempt
- Shalako
- Spirits of the Dead

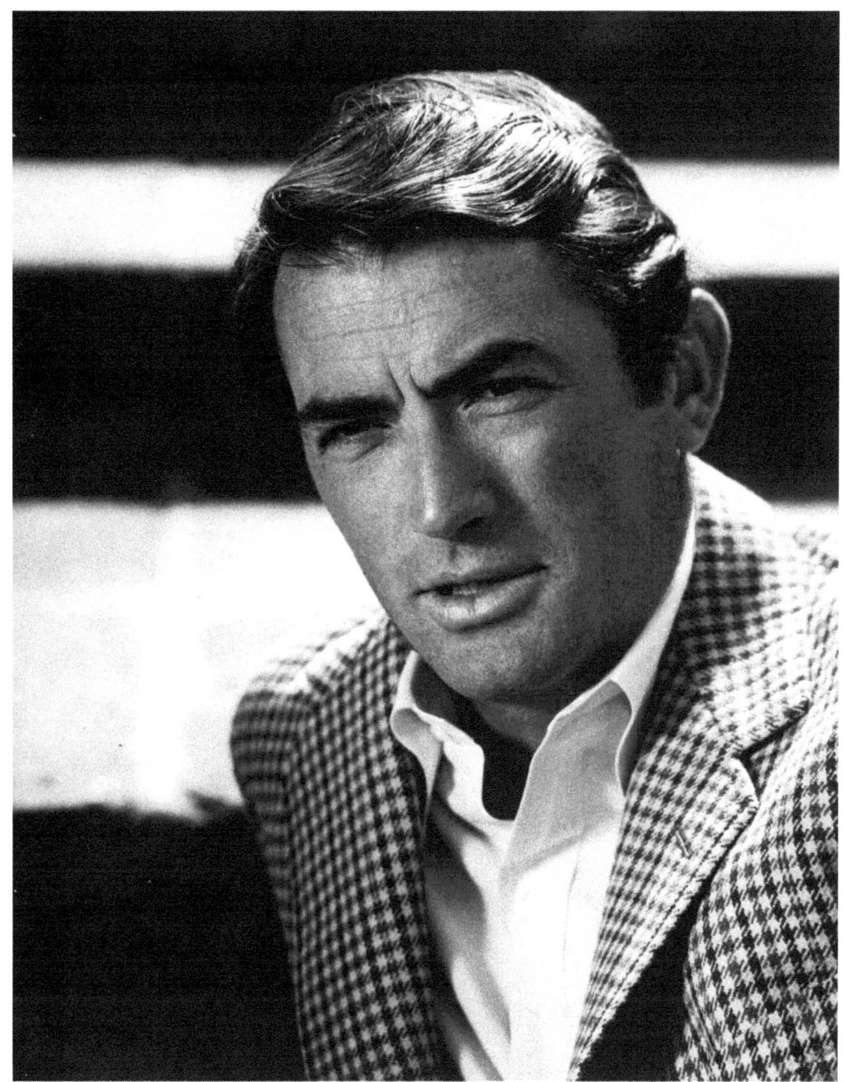

Gregory Peck

Movies:

- Spellbound
- Duel In The Sun
- The Yearling
- Roman Holiday

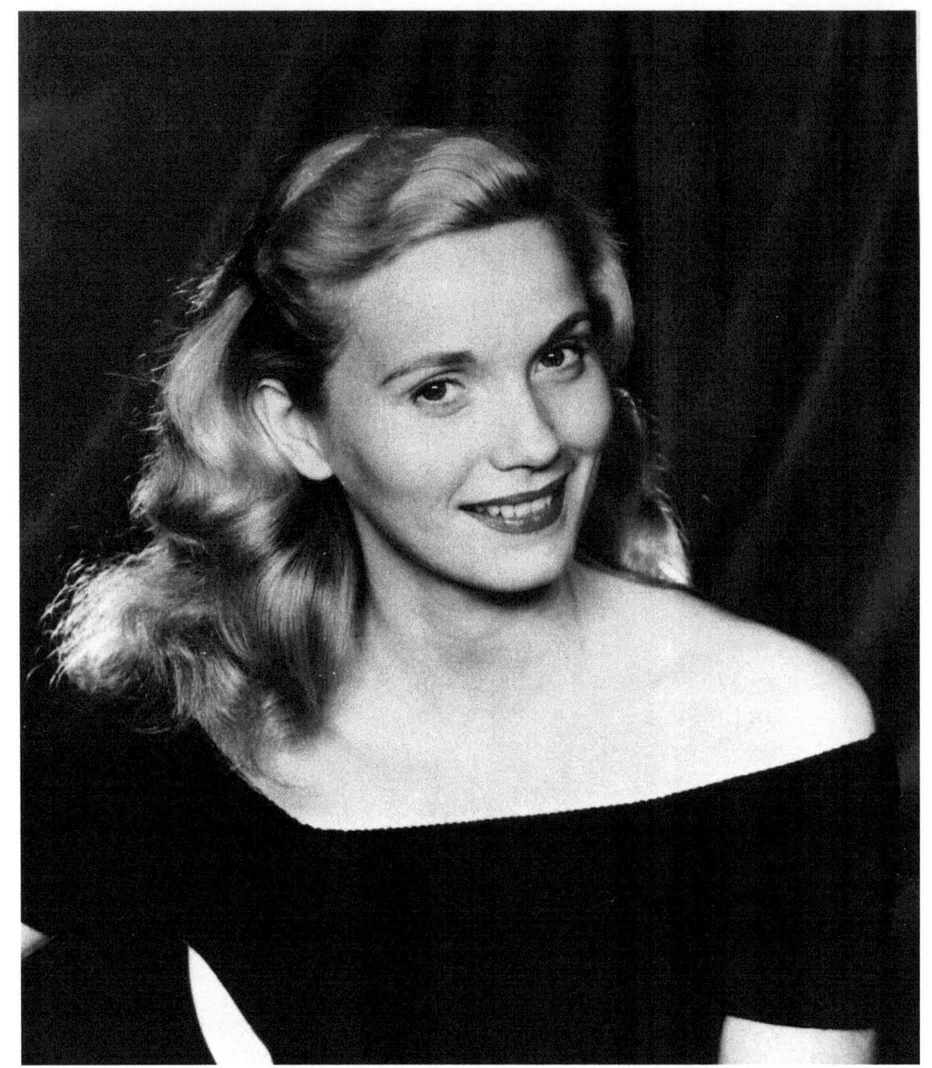

Eva Marie Saint

Movies:

- North by Northwest
- Exodus
- On the Waterfront
- Grand Prix

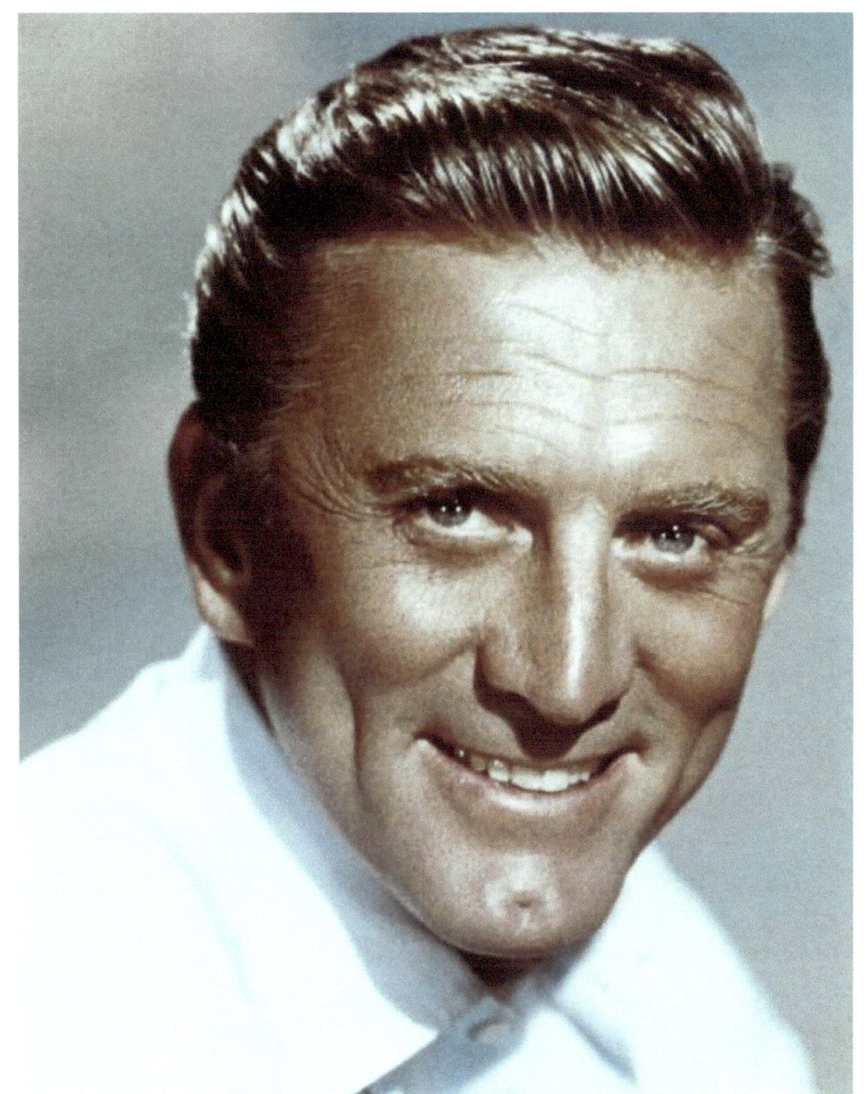

Kirk Douglas

Movies:

- Champion
- Ace in the Hole
- Detective Story
- Lust for Life

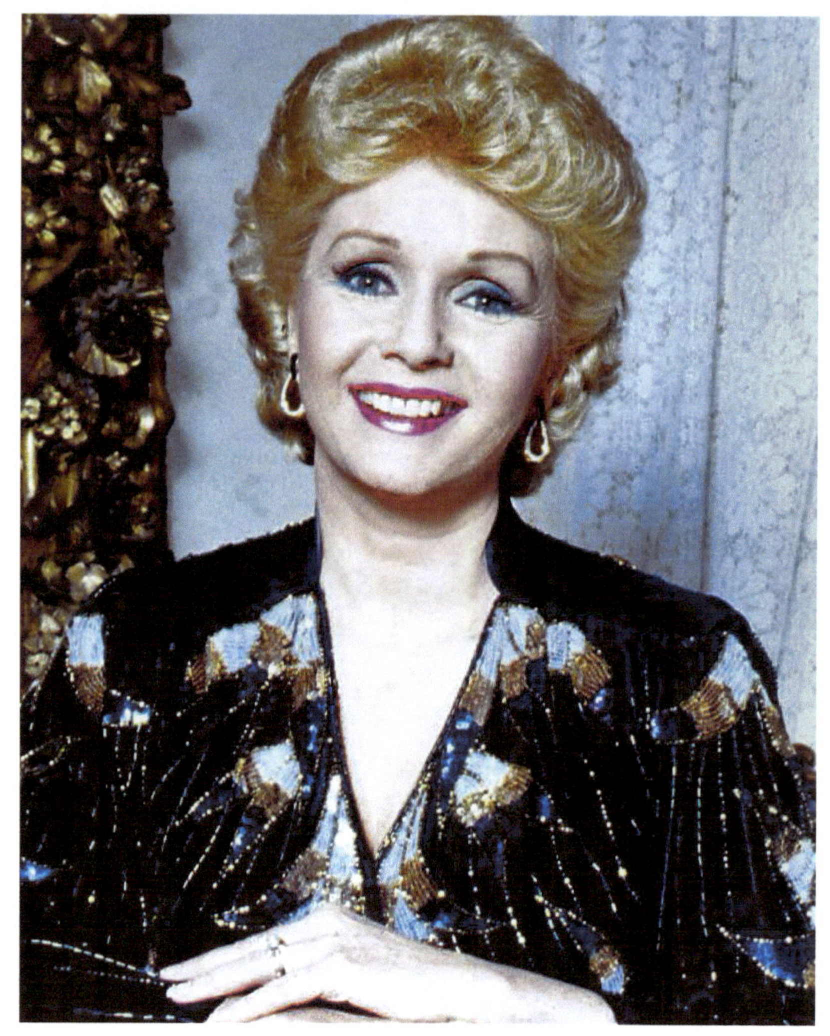

Debbie Reynolds

Movies:

- Singin' in the Rain
- Charlotte's Web
- How the West Was Won
- In & Out

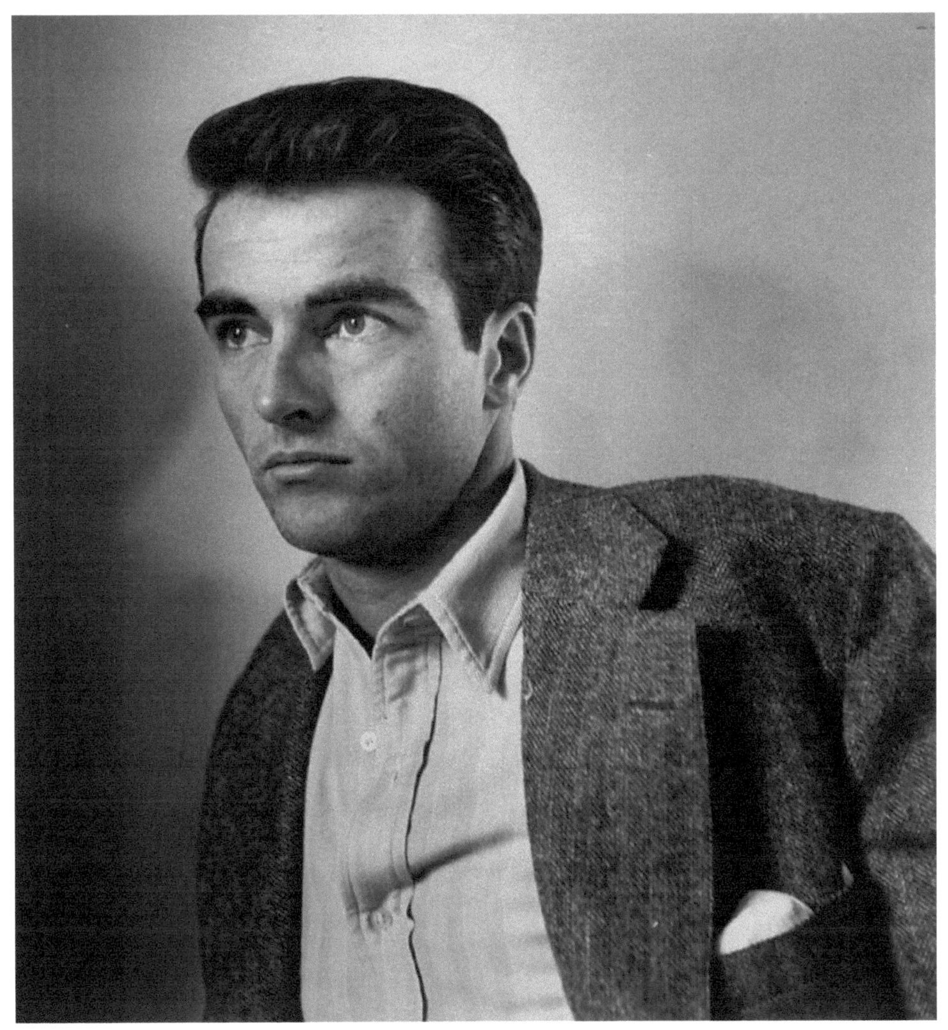

Montgomery Clift

Movies:

- Red River
- Judgment at Nuremberg
- From Here To Eternity
- The Heiress

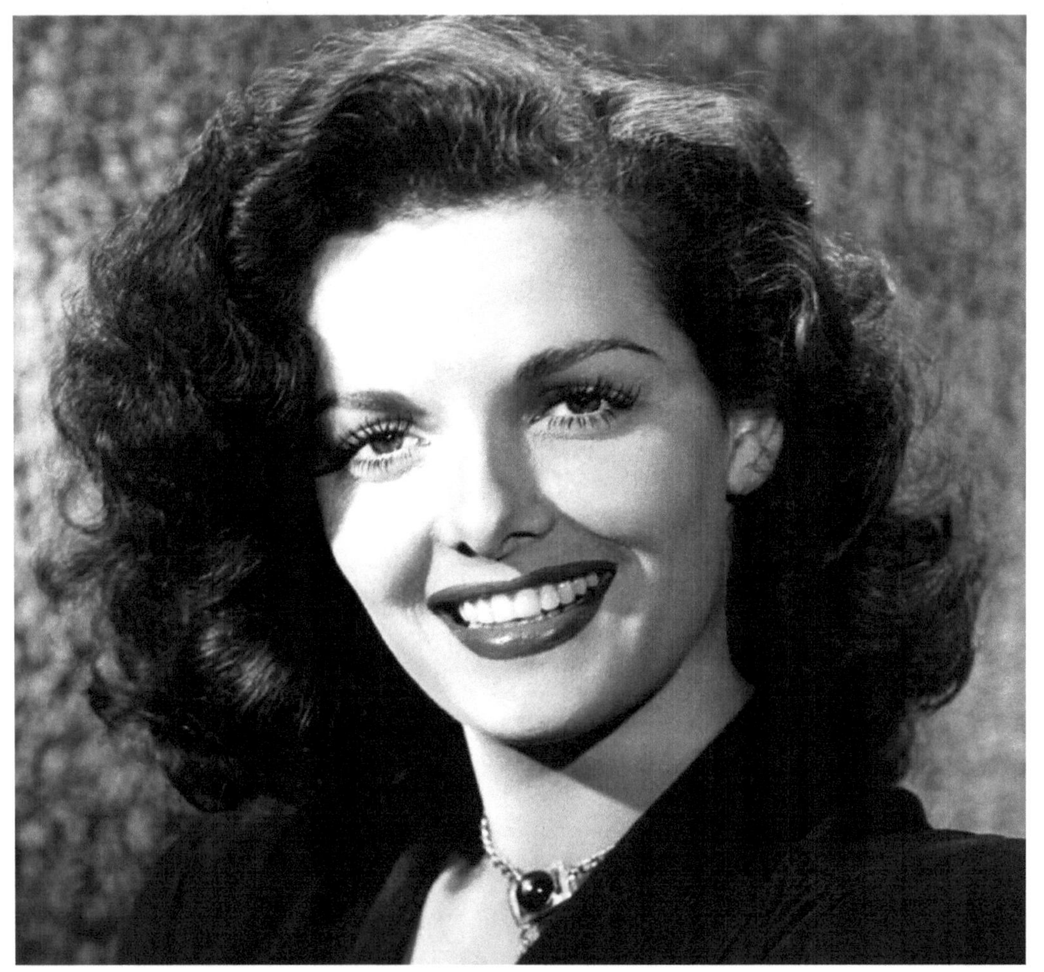

Jane Russell

Movies:

- Cinema Paradiso
- The Born Losers
- The Outlaw
- Road to Bali

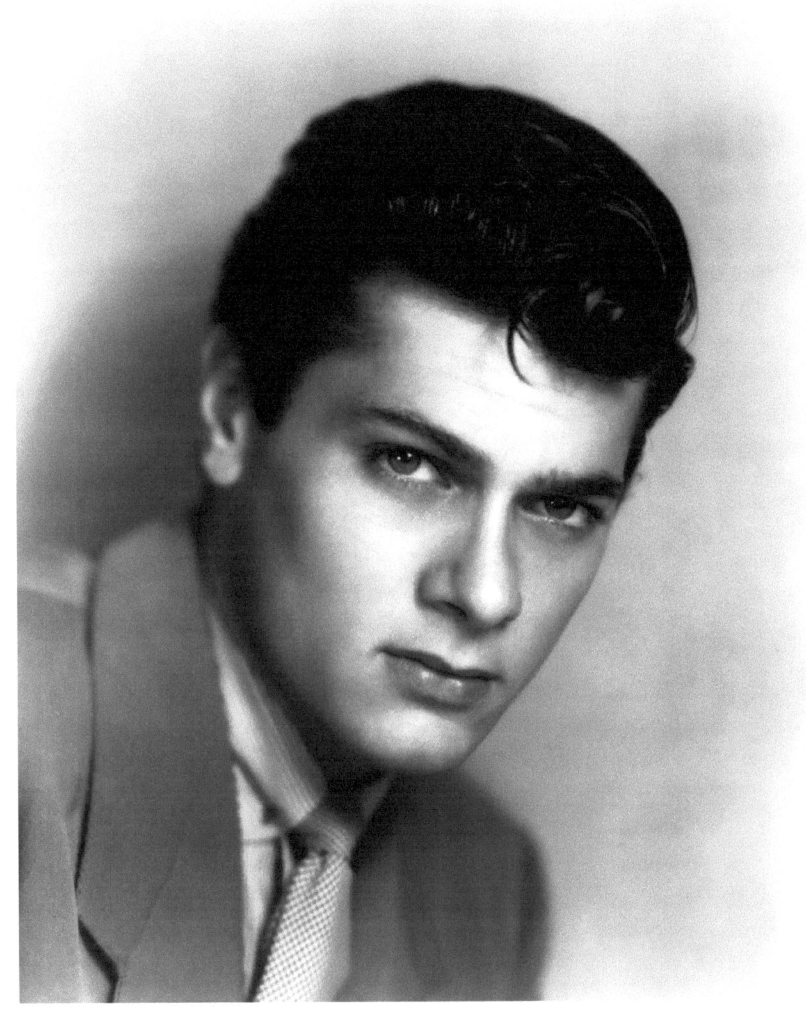

Tony Curtis

Movies:

- Some Like It Hot
- Trapeze
- Francis
- The Defiant Ones

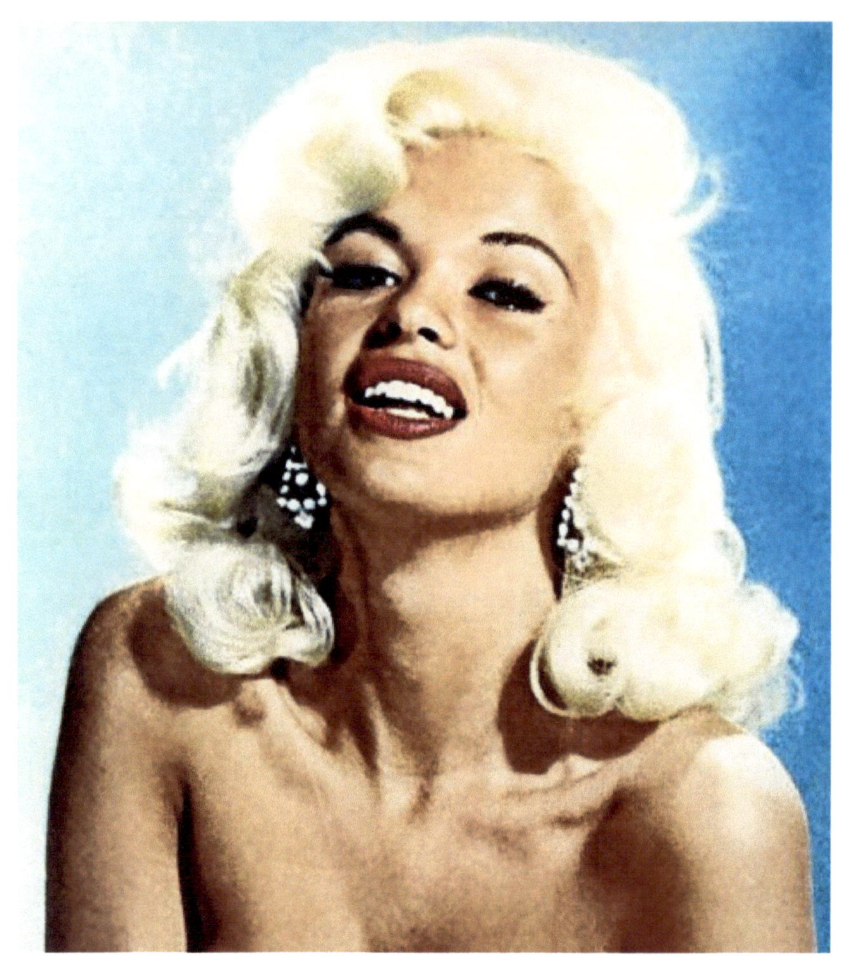

Jayne Mansfield

Movies:

- The Fat Spy
- The Girl Can't Help It
- Hell on Frisco Bay
- The Burglar

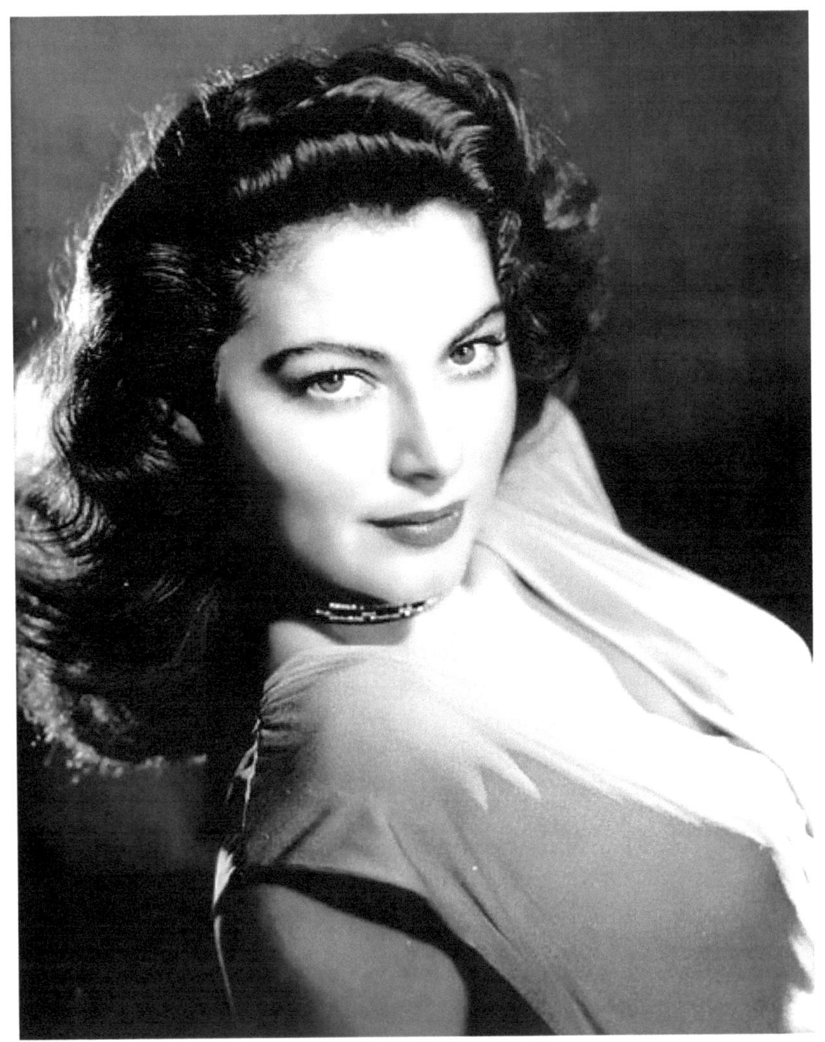

Ava Gardner

Movies:

- The Killers
- Show Boat
- The Hucksters
- On The Beach

Acknowledgement

Page No. I Author/s I Title I Source I License

James Stewart I kate gabrielle (slightlyterrific)
James Stewart I https://www.flickr.com/photos/slightlyterrific/5365664482/
Attribution 2.0 Generic (CC BY 2.0)

John Wayne I Silver Screen
John Wayne 1907-1979 I https://www.flickr.com/photos/123723459@N07/25476761804/
Public Domain Mark 1.0

Charlton Heston I Silver Screen
Charlton_Heston I https://www.flickr.com/photos/123723459@N07/25521196094/
Public Domain Mark 1.0

Marlon Brando Ur Cameras
Marlon Brando - The Wild One I https://www.flickr.com/photos/136879256@N02/24786321832/
Public Domain Mark 1.0

William Holden I kate gabrielle (slightlyterrific)
William Holden I https://www.flickr.com/photos/slightlyterrific/5190363883/
Attribution 2.0 Generic (CC BY 2.0)

Marilyn Monroe I Rokr Rafterson
(raftrokr) Marilyn Monroe I https://www.flickr.com/photos/raftrokr/439127733/
Attribution-ShareAlike 2.0 Generic (CC BY-SA 2.0)

Shirley MacLaine I Film Star Vintage (classicvintage)
Shirley MacLaine I https://www.flickr.com/photos/classicvintage/9382480298/
Attribution 2.0 Generic (CC BY 2.0)

Rock Hudson I Insomnia Cured Here (tom-margie)
Rock Hudson I https://www.flickr.com/photos/tom-margie/1552111179/
Attribution-ShareAlike 2.0 Generic (CC BY-SA 2.0)

Clark Gable Insomnia Cured Here (tom-margie)
Clark Gable I https://www.flickr.com/photos/tom-margie/1556055469/
Attribution-ShareAlike 2.0 Generic (CC BY-SA 2.0)

Audrey Hepburn I Nicholas R. Andrew (Nicholas Andrew)
Audrey Hepburn smoking 7 I https://www.flickr.com/photos/9355127@N07/4509041656/
Public Domain Mark 1.0

Jerry Lewis I John Mathew Smith & www.celebrity-photos.com (kingkongphoto)
Jerry Lewis I https://www.flickr.com/photos/kingkongphoto/5112583711/
Attribution-ShareAlike 2.0 Generic (CC BY-SA 2.0)

Elizabeth Taylor I Pipe Loyola M
Elizabeth Taylor I https://www.flickr.com/photos/solo_antonio/5587360422/
Attribution 2.0 Generic (CC BY 2.0)

Burt Lancaster I kate gabrielle (slightlyterrific)
Burt Lancaster I https://www.flickr.com/photos/slightlyterrific/5351366148/
Attribution 2.0 Generic (CC BY 2.0)

Grace Kelly I Pierre Tourigny (manitou2121)
Grace Kelly I https://www.flickr.com/photos/pierre_tourigny/3856922160/
Attribution 2.0 Generic (CC BY 2.0)

Frank Sinatra I Insomnia Cured Here (tom-margie)
Frank Sinatra I https://www.flickr.com/photos/tom-margie/1547214740/
Attribution-ShareAlike 2.0 Generic (CC BY-SA 2.0)

Dean Martin I Lawren (MrBlueGenes)
Martin, Dean - Dean Martin Christmas Album, The
https://www.flickr.com/photos/mrbluegenes/5221942527/
Attribution 2.0 Generic (CC BY 2.0)

Sophia Loren I Pierre Tourigny (manitou2121)
Sophia Loren I https://www.flickr.com/photos/pierre_tourigny/3856928234/
Attribution 2.0 Generic (CC BY 2.0)

Gary CooperI kate gabrielle (slightlyterrific)
Gary Cooper I https://www.flickr.com/photos/slightlyterrific/5348069606/
Attribution 2.0 Generic (CC BY 2.0)

Kim Novak I kate gabrielle (slightlyterrific)
Kim Novak I https://www.flickr.com/photos/slightlyterrific/5347440031/
Attribution 2.0 Generic (CC BY 2.0)

James Dean I Affluent.Recluse
James Dean I https://www.flickr.com/photos/48386506@N06/4886583472/
Public Domain Mark 1.0

Natalie Wood I Film Star Vintage (classicvintage)
Natalie Wood I https://www.flickr.com/photos/classicvintage/9281336842/
Attribution 2.0 Generic (CC BY 2.0)

Humphrey Bogart I Insomnia Cured Here (tom-margie)
Humphrey Bogart I https://www.flickr.com/photos/tom-margie/1547212828/
Attribution-ShareAlike 2.0 Generic (CC BY-SA 2.0)

Doris Day I kate gabrielle (slightlyterrific)
Doris Day I https://www.flickr.com/photos/slightlyterrific/5350792089/
Attribution 2.0 Generic (CC BY 2.0)

Jack Lemmon I kate gabrielle (slightlyterrific)
Jack Lemmon I https://www.flickr.com/photos/slightlyterrific/5190348459/
Attribution 2.0 Generic (CC BY 2.0)

Susan Hayward I Pierre Tourigny (manitou2121)
Susan Hayward I https://www.flickr.com/photos/pierre_tourigny/3856134523/
Attribution 2.0 Generic (CC BY 2.0)

Glenn Ford I kate gabrielle (slightlyterrific)
Glenn Ford I https://www.flickr.com/photos/slightlyterrific/5190954834/
Attribution 2.0 Generic (CC BY 2.0)

Deborah Kerr I Susanlenox
Deborah Kerr (1921- Oct 16 2007)I https://www.flickr.com/photos/jumborois/2946524161/
Public Domain Mark 1.0

Cary GrantI kate gabrielle (slightlyterrific)
Cary Grant I https://www.flickr.com/photos/slightlyterrific/5350782927/
Attribution 2.0 Generic (CC BY 2.0)

Lucille Ball I AustinMini1275
Lucille Ball I https://www.flickr.com/photos/14639118@N03/26302339438/
Public Domain Mark 1.0

Elvis Presley I Brett JordanI
Elvis Is Back! I https://www.flickr.com/photos/x1brett/8341831089/
Attribution 2.0 Generic (CC BY 2.0)

Brigitte BardotI jbde I Brigitte Bardot
https://www.flickr.com/photos/146038987@N08/33180695243/
Public Domain Mark 1.0

Gregory Peck I kate gabrielle (slightlyterrific)
Gregory Peck I https://www.flickr.com/photos/slightlyterrific/5190961714
Attribution 2.0 Generic (CC BY 2.0)

Eva Marie Saint I kate gabrielle (slightlyterrific)
Eva Marie Saint I https://www.flickr.com/photos/slightlyterrific/5190344883/
Attribution 2.0 Generic (CC BY 2.0)

Kirk Douglas I monstersforsale
Kirk Douglas I https://www.flickr.com/photos/51514834@N00/38942456732/
Public Domain Mark 1.0

Debbie Reynolds I Furn Class (Furnly)
Debbie_Reynolds-sitting I https://www.flickr.com/photos/146553050@N07/31855140801/
Attribution-ShareAlike 2.0 Generic (CC BY-SA 2.0)

Montgomery Clift I Film Star Vintage (classicvintage)
Montgomery Clift I https://www.flickr.com/photos/classicvintage/9363564374/
Attribution 2.0 Generic (CC BY 2.0)

Jane Russell I Silver Screen
Jane_Russell I https://www.flickr.com/photos/123723459@N07/26052607512/
Public Domain Mark 1.0

Tony Curtis I Insomnia Cured Here (tom-margie)
Tony Curtis I https://www.flickr.com/photos/tom-margie/1548813614/
Attribution-ShareAlike 2.0 Generic (CC BY-SA 2.0)

Jayne Mansfield I AustinMini1275 I Jayne Mansfield
https://www.flickr.com/photos/14639118@N03/29186249667
Public Domain Mark 1.0

Ava Gardner I Insomnia Cured Here (tom-margie)
Ava Gardner https://www.flickr.com/photos/tom-margie/1549461280/ Attribution-ShareAlike 2.0
Generic (CC BY-SA 2.0)

www.ingramcontent.com/pod-product-compliance
Ingram Content Group UK Ltd.
Pitfield, Milton Keynes, MK11 3LW, UK
UKHW060111300726
14090UKWH00002B/139